THE SUN WILL COME UP TOMORROW

Finding Happiness at Life's Stops Along the Way

Jim Petersen, PhD

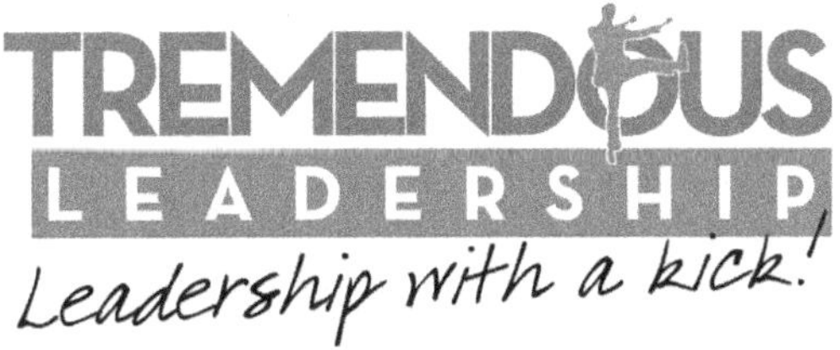

Published by: Executive Books | Tremendous Life Books
P.O. Box 267, Boiling Springs, PA 17007 717-701-8159 | 800-233-2665
www.TremendousLeadership.com

Paperback ISBN: 978-1-961202-80-1
Ebook ISBN: 978-1-961202-81-8

FOREWORD

I have known Jim Petersen for forty years, and known him well, a distinction that matters. Many people know Jim from a distance, from his books, his speaking platform, his reputation in leadership and coaching circles. I have known him up close, across four decades of close friendship, and what I can tell you is that the man you will meet in these pages is the same man who shows up in every other room of his life.

Such consistency is rare.

Jim's path is, by any measure, remarkable. He graduated from the United States Naval Academy and went on to master the demanding world of nuclear submarine operations, a domain that accepts no performance and no pretense, only competence and character. He excelled in the financial services industry for more than three decades, ultimately reaching the highest levels of executive leadership. He shifted then into teaching and coaching, where he has built one of the most respected practices in that field and where he continues, to this day, to develop leaders who go on to develop others.

That résumé would be enough for most people. Jim has never treated it as enough.

What defines Jim Petersen is not the accolades, though the accolades are real and earned. What defines him is the pursuit, the sustained, still-growing passion for life, for the people around him, for the question of how a person actually lives well rather than simply succeeds. He is a devoted husband, a father, and a grandfather who invests in those relationships with the same intentionality he brings to everything else. I have watched him use his time, his talent, and his treasure in the service of other people for four decades. It is not a pose. It is who he is.

That is the person who wrote this book, and that is why this book is worth reading.

In *The Sun Will Come Up Tomorrow: Finding Happiness at Life's Stops Along the Way*, Jim explores what most of us are quietly looking for: happiness that holds, purpose that sustains, and the kind of joy that does not depend on everything going right. He does not offer a formula. He offers something better, stories drawn from a life fully lived, hard-won reflections from someone who has been through the stops he is writing about, and the particular wisdom of a man who has been happy not because his life has been easy but because he has learned, over a long time and through genuine difficulty, how to choose happiness as a practice rather than wait for it as a reward.

I have seen this philosophy at work in Jim's life for forty years. I have watched it sustain him through the difficult seasons and deepen him through the good ones. I am glad he finally wrote it down.

Read this book. You will be richer for it, in every sense of the word.

Lamar C. Smith
Former Chief Executive Officer
Decorated Combat Pilot
Coach to Executives

DEDICATION

To my wife, Louise, and to our children and grandchildren, who remind me every day that life's greatest happiness is found in the people we love.

TABLE OF CONTENTS

INTRODUCTION

There is a phrase I have been saying for most of my adult life. I said it to a friend's wife many years ago when she was deep in worry about things she could not control, and it has traveled with me ever since, through career changes and family milestones, through losses and surprises, through the full, unpredictable arc of a life I could not have designed from the starting line.

The sun will come up tomorrow.

It sounds simple because it is. That is the point.

This book was born from a lifetime of watching people search for happiness in the wrong places, at the wrong times, by the wrong measures. It was also born from watching the same people stumble upon something real and lasting in the moments they least expected it, at a stop they didn't plan, in the middle of a life that wasn't following the script.

The Woman Who Worried About Everything

Many years ago, I became close friends with one of the salespeople I had hired, and over time, I also came to know his wife well. I was, and have always been, a very positive person. She was very much the opposite. She worried about almost everything.

Her worries were not unusual. Like many parents, she worried about whether her husband's sales career would provide enough income, whether her children would attend the right schools, and whether they would live in the right neighborhood. The future, for her, was something that needed to be managed and prepared for rather than simply lived toward.

One afternoon, after hearing another round of anxious speculation, I simply said: "The sun will come up tomorrow."

At first, the statement seemed dismissive. Yet over time, the phrase began to stick. Whenever worry surfaced, she would laugh and say it herself. It became a kind of touchstone, a small reminder that the world would continue turning regardless of what the worried mind had constructed overnight.

Life eventually took turns she never expected. Her marriage ended. A second marriage later failed as well. And yet her children grew up to build remarkable lives. One became an FBI agent. Another became a military pilot who later flew commercial aircraft. Her youngest daughter built a loving family of her own.

Years later, she moved near her grandchildren and discovered something she once feared she might never experience: peace. Her life did not follow the plan she had imagined. But happiness arrived anyway. I am very proud of her for navigating through life's challenges to find a fulfilled life on the other side. Many of the things we worry about never define our lives. What defines us is how we move through them.

A Reflection Before We Begin

The decision to write this book was inspired by someone else.

From time to time, people ask when I plan to write my next book. Recently, I came to the conclusion that five books were probably enough. I didn't have another topic in mind and, frankly, I had plenty of other obligations competing for my time.

My usual answer became simple: not in the near future, unless there is a sequel to something I have already written.

Then someone asked me a slightly different question.

They said, "When will you write your next book? You should write a book about happiness. You are one of the happiest people I know."

At the time, I was extremely busy, so I politely set the idea aside. I simply didn't have the time to give a new book the attention it deserved. But ideas have a way of lingering in the background, even when we try to ignore them.

During a quiet moment of reflection, I asked myself a simple question: if you were going to write a book about happiness, what would you call it? That question opened a door I hadn't expected. As I thought about the title, I also began thinking about a deeper question: why am I happy? The answer didn't arrive all at once. In fact, after that brief moment of reflection, I dropped the subject entirely because I knew it would consume my time. Life moved on.

But a couple of months later, something interesting happened. I woke up very early one morning with a stream of ideas running through my mind: how the book might be structured, what themes it might explore, and how the stories might unfold. I quickly went to my computer to capture those thoughts before they disappeared like so many early-morning reflections tend to do. Before I knew it, I was off to the races, working on a book that I had previously convinced myself I wasn't going to write.

My problem, and perhaps my strength, is that I tend to accept challenges when they present themselves, especially if they might help someone live a better life.

I did not write this book alone. Two exceptional AI companions, Perfecto and Claude, helped me develop the ideas, find the stories, and shape the material into something worth reading. My publisher, Tracey Jones, provided the insight, encouragement, and professional guidance that every author needs and not every author is fortunate enough to have. I am grateful to all three.

This book focuses on what people can do to experience a happy and prosperous life. It is not a traditional self-help book with a list of steps that promise happiness if followed perfectly. Life rarely works that way.

Life has a way of sending us messages, some that contribute to our happiness and some that detract from it. Taken together, these experiences often influence how we feel about our lives. But I have come to believe something slightly different. I believe that life is full of choices. We get to choose.

Consider the classic example of a glass filled halfway with liquid. Some people see the glass as half empty. Others see it as half full. The situation itself is identical, yet the interpretation is completely different. Many situations in life are like that glass.

Some people don't realize they have a choice in how they interpret those moments. They simply allow events to shape their outlook. Over time, that outlook can become either optimistic or pessimistic without much conscious thought.

Personally, I try to see the glass as half full most of the time. That does not mean ignoring reality. Some situations genuinely lean one direction or the other, and there are circumstances we simply cannot control. I accept those. But in the situations where perspective matters, and there are many, I choose to look for the positive side.

Occasionally, people say to me that it must be easy for me to be happy because I have had success in life. When they say that, I often respond with a question: Did I become successful and then become happy? Or was I happy first, and that happiness contributed to my success?

For me, the answer is the latter.

Happy Before Success

When I say I believe I was happy before I was successful, it requires explanation. I am more of a giver than a taker, although I could have been both. I enjoyed having opportunities to grow, and that contributed to my happiness. I did not need something in return, but I was grateful for what I received.

I was competitive. I still am. I wanted to excel at the Naval Academy. I wanted to qualify in submarines. I wanted to be ranked first among the instructors at Nuclear Power School. I wanted to build a meaningful career in financial services, to lead well, and to be respected by the people I worked alongside. These were not small ambitions, and the satisfaction of pursuing them was genuine and important to me.

But I was also, through most of that pursuit, genuinely happy. And when I ask myself why, I keep arriving at the same three answers.

The first is that I was engaged. I was doing things that required everything I had, academically, physically, and professionally, and there is a particular quality of happiness that comes from being fully stretched by something you care about. It is not the happiness of comfort. It is the happiness of being completely alive with what is in front of you.

The second is that I had people. My wife. My children, as they arrived. My crew on the submarine, my family, and my friends who became my people in the fullest sense of that word. The relationships that would sustain everything else were built during the years when the resume was still modest. I did not know then what the research would later confirm: that the quality of our relationships predicts our happiness more reliably than almost anything else. I only knew that I was surrounded by people I cared about and who cared about me, and that this made the hard things manageable and the good things genuinely joyful.

The third is that the work meant something. Even before the titles and the recognition, I was doing work that mattered to people beyond myself, serving my country, developing young officers, and eventually helping families build financial security. Teaching the brightest minds of the future. Purpose was present long before prestige arrived.

I think those three things, engagement, relationships, and purpose, are what made me happy before success came. And the reason I share this is not to tell a story about myself. It is because those three things are available to you right now, regardless of where you are in the arc of your career or your life. They do not require a corner office, a title, or a number in a bank account. They require attention and intention, which are things you can choose today.

That is the argument this book is making. And I know it is true because I lived it in the wrong order: happiness first, then success. And the happiness came from exactly the places this book is going to take you.

Most organizations want happy employees. Positive people tend to create positive environments, and those environments often lead to better outcomes. The same is true in families.

When people look at our family today, they sometimes say that everything turned out well, as if it happened overnight. But that outcome was the result of years of effort and care, especially from my wife, who invested an enormous amount of time raising our children and guiding them toward becoming productive, thoughtful adults. Today, we are grateful that they have built families of their own with spouses they love. Watching those families grow continues to bring us tremendous joy.

This book can be read straight through, and I hope it will be. It can also be revisited later, chapter by chapter, when life presents the particular stop, setback, or season that makes a certain lesson newly relevant.

An analogy I learned many years ago may help explain this idea. Someone once said: Shoot for the moon. If you fall short, you will still land among the stars. I took that to mean that failure is not something to fear. We do not have to hit every target we aim for in life. Sometimes when we miss the mark, we end up somewhere unexpected, yet equally meaningful. Life has a way of doing that.

For readers who want to understand how this book connects to the Petersen Leadership Framework and the three books that preceded it, an appendix at the back explains the full picture. It is there when you want it and easy to find when you do.

A Closing Reflection

Over time, I have come to think of happiness in a very simple way.

Happiness is a lot like sunshine.

Some days the sun is bright and obvious. Everything feels warm and clear, and it is easy to appreciate the light around us. On other days, the sky is covered with clouds. The sun is still there, but we cannot always see it.

Life works much the same way.

There are seasons when everything seems to be going well: family, career, friendships, health, and opportunities all appear to align. During those times, happiness seems natural and effortless.

But there are also days when clouds move in. Disappointments happen. Plans fail. People we care about struggle. Circumstances change in ways we cannot control.

The sunshine has not disappeared. It is simply harder to see.

One of the ideas explored throughout this book is that happiness is not something we wait for. It is something we learn to recognize, nurture, and sometimes choose even when the clouds are present. Sunshine does not eliminate storms, but it reminds us that storms do not last forever.

My hope is not to tell you how to live your life. Instead, my hope is that something in these pages helps you notice the sunshine that may already be present in your life or encourages you to look for it when the clouds appear.

Because in the end, happiness is not reserved for a fortunate few. It is something all of us can experience. Sometimes we just have to remember to look toward the light.

This book is organized into four parts, each one representing a different season of a life in progress. Part One examines the ideas we carry about happiness and how they often work against us. Part Two follows a life through its most significant stops, from early work and family to the unexpected detours that redirect everything. Part Three explores the qualities that drive lasting happiness, beginning with five that matter most: perspective, relationships, purpose, gratitude, and resilience, and extending into the equally important territory of humor and service. Part Four considers what happiness looks like when we arrive somewhere we didn't plan to be, watching our children succeed, becoming grandparents, and discovering that the best chapter was the one we hadn't written yet.

Each chapter contains stories. Some are mine. They are drawn from a life that has taken me from a naval submarine to a university classroom to an executive coaching practice, from a blizzard birth in Connecticut to a private club dinner with a daughter who did not yet know what was waiting for her in a statement on the table. I tell those stories in my own voice, with the specific detail that only a participant can provide, and I stand behind every one of them.

Other stories belong to people I have known, coached, and learned from, or to composite characters built from patterns I have observed across decades of working closely with leaders, families, and individuals navigating the full range of what life sends. These third-party stories are told in a more novelistic voice, with named characters and fully developed scenes, because that form is the most honest way to transmit what I witnessed. The names and identifying details have been changed or composited to protect privacy. The experiences and the lessons are real.

The two kinds of story ask slightly different things of the reader. The personal ones ask you to trust that I am telling the truth about my own life, which I am. The third-party ones ask you to recognize yourself or someone you know in the situation, which most readers do. In every case, the stories are true in the way that matters most: they happened to real people, in real circumstances, and they carry lessons that do not require the specific details to be yours for the meaning to land.

The sun will come up tomorrow. It always has. It always will.

What we choose to do with the day it illuminates is the whole story.

Part I

THE FOUNDATION OF HAPPINESS

What we believe about happiness,
and why it often isn't true

Chapter 1

THE HAPPINESS ILLUSION

Ask most people what would make them happy, and they will answer without hesitation. A raise. A promotion. The house they have been saving toward. The relationship that finally works the way they always imagined it could. The list is specific, reasonable, and almost always organized around things that have not yet arrived.

This is the happiness illusion: the belief, held sincerely and almost universally, that happiness exists just past the next milestone. Get the thing, feel the feeling. It is a sensible theory. It is also, as a remarkable body of research and an even more remarkable collection of human experience suggests, largely wrong.

Many people believe happiness will arrive when they achieve the next milestone: a promotion, financial success, recognition, or security. Yet when those milestones arrive, the feeling often fades quickly. What once seemed extraordinary becomes ordinary within weeks. Psychologists call this hedonic adaptation, the tendency of humans to return to a stable level of happiness despite major positive or negative events.

We are, in other words, remarkably good at returning to baseline. The raise feels significant until it becomes the new normal. The house that was a dream becomes the house that needs a new roof. The relationship that seemed perfect becomes the relationship that requires work.

Happiness is not a destination waiting at the end of a perfect plan. It is something we discover along the journey, most often at the stops we didn't schedule. This chapter is about what happens when we treat it as a destination, and what becomes possible when we stop.

The Horizon Line

Marcus had one goal: to make partner.

For more than a decade, he arrived before the sun and left after it. He skipped his daughter's recital once, just once, he told himself, because the Hendricks account was on the line. He told his wife, "Once I make partner, I'll have more say over my schedule. We'll take that trip to Portugal. I'll coach Emma's soccer team. Just a little longer."

The day the letter came, he poured two fingers of bourbon and sat quietly for twenty minutes. Then his phone buzzed. A message from the managing director: Congrats. You'll want to start thinking about your path to senior partner. Marcus set down the glass.

It wasn't that the goal had been wrong. It was that he had treated happiness like a destination on a map, something you arrive at. But the horizon doesn't work that way. You walk toward it, and it walks with you.

He thought about a phrase his old football coach used to say: "The scoreboard never tells you who you are, only where you've been." The partner title told him where he'd been. It said nothing about where he was going or who he wanted to be when he got there.

He called his wife. "Do you still want to go to Portugal?"

She paused. "I thought you'd never ask."

"I almost didn't," he said.

Lesson

The story works because it's not about ambition being bad. Marcus's drive was real and earned something real. The shift is in the relationship with the goal. When the goal is the condition for happiness rather than a waypoint through it, we end up postponing our own lives.

The goalpost doesn't move on its own, we move it, because arriving would mean having to decide who we are now. Sometimes the chase is the hiding. Ask yourself: What are you waiting to accomplish before you allow yourself to be happy? And what is that waiting costing you today?

The Corner Office

Richard wanted the corner office for eleven years.

Not in the vague, ambient way that most people want things they know they probably won't get. He wanted it specifically, the particular office on the fourteenth floor of the building he had worked in since his thirty-first year, the one with two walls of glass and a view that looked south toward the river. He had walked past it hundreds of times. He had noticed, without meaning to, when the previous occupant rearranged the furniture. He had stood in the doorway once, during a facilities walkthrough nobody else cared about, and measured the room in footsteps while pretending to look at the ceiling tiles.

He was not a vain man. He understood that wanting an office was not the same as having a vision. But the corner office had become, over eleven years, the concrete symbol of the thing he actually wanted, which was the acknowledgment that he earned his place, that the people above him finally saw what he brought to the organization since the year he arrived, that the long, patient, occasionally grinding work of building something excellent had been noticed and valued.

The promotion came on a Tuesday in March. His name on the door was installed by Thursday. On Friday morning, he arrived early, before anyone else, and stood in the room alone in the particular quality of light that the south-facing windows produced at that hour; and waited.

He waited for the feeling he had imagined for eleven years.

It arrived. It was genuine, warm, and real. He is clear about this when he tells the story; he is not describing a disappointment that announced itself immediately. He felt good. He felt proud. He felt, for several days, the specific satisfaction of a man who has climbed something and is now standing at the top.

And then, somewhere in the second week, he noticed that he was exactly himself.

Not a different version of himself, not an elevated version, not the version of himself that the corner office was supposed to confirm and unlock. Just himself, sitting in a nicer chair, with a better view of the river, carrying the same unresolved questions he always carried about whether he was doing enough, whether he was respected in the ways that actually mattered, whether the work he was doing was the work he was supposed to be doing with the years he left.

The office had not answered any of those questions. He assumed, without ever stating the assumption to himself directly, that it would. That the external confirmation would settle something internal. It hadn't. It had simply given the questions a nicer backdrop.

He tells this story now to the people he manages, particularly the ones he can see organizing their ambitions around a single visible prize: the title, the team size, the budget number, the recognition at the annual meeting. He doesn't tell it to deflate them. He tells it because he wishes someone had told it to him eleven years earlier, not to talk him out of working hard, but to suggest that the thing he was really looking for was not located where he was looking for it.

"The corner office is real," he tells them. "Work for it if you want it. Just don't put it in charge of how you feel about yourself. It doesn't know how to do that job, and when it disappoints you, and it will disappoint you, not because it's bad but because it's just a room, you'll be standing there wondering why the thing you wanted for eleven years isn't doing what you needed it to do."

Most of them nod in the way that people nod when they understand something intellectually and have not yet lived it. He nods back. He understands. He did the same thing.

The lesson Richard eventually articulated for himself was not that ambition is wrong or that external goals are meaningless. It was something more precise: the feeling he had been waiting for, the settled sense of being enough, was never going to be delivered by anything outside of him. It lived inside him, or it didn't live at all, and the corner office was never going to be the address.

What shifted for Richard, in the months after he moved into that room, was not his ambition but his relationship to it. He kept working hard. He kept wanting things. But he started being more honest with himself about what he was really asking about those things to do for him, and whether they were capable of doing it.

The view of the river is still there every morning. He genuinely likes it. He no longer needs it to mean anything beyond what it is. That, it turned out, is when he finally got what he had actually been looking for.

Chapter 2

THE COMPARISON TRAP

The comparison trap is more subtle than the happiness illusion because it rarely arrives looking like envy. It arrives looking like information: someone else's title, someone else's house, someone else's marriage. Someone else's child who appears to be thriving in all the ways ours are not currently demonstrating. We look sideways, gather the data, and quietly alter our emotional weather without ever admitting that comparison was the instrument doing the altering.

Comparison is one of the fastest ways to drain joy from a perfectly good life. Not because it tells us nothing true, but because it tells us truth without context. It shows us outcomes without costs, surfaces without structure, the visible result without the invisible burden that came attached to it. Most people are not comparing their actual lives to another person's actual life. They are comparing their actual life to a curated excerpt.

There is a reason comparison has such a powerful effect on happiness. Human beings are social creatures, and social creatures are constantly locating themselves in relation to other people. That instinct was probably useful when survival depended on reading status, belonging, and proximity to the tribe. It is far less useful when it is applied to social media, neighborhood economics, school admissions, or professional titles.

The result is a life lived by borrowed scorecards.

One person compares salaries. Another compares appearance. Another compares the visible behavior of a teenager on a college visit and concludes something sweeping about their own child. Another attends a reunion and comes home strangely dissatisfied with a life they had been perfectly content with two hours earlier. Nothing in their actual life changed during the evening. Only the measuring instrument did.

The Reunion Table

At class reunions, there is always a brief and revealing period in which everyone pretends not to be comparing while clearly comparing. The questions are polite enough. What are you doing now? Where are you living? How are the kids? The tone is warm, the smiles are real, and yet under the surface, a different conversation is running. Who did better? Who married well? Who looks tired? Who seems to have landed where the rest of us hoped to land?

I have watched this dynamic enough times to know that the happiest people at those tables are usually not the ones with the most impressive answers. They are the ones least interested in using the table as a ranking system. They are curious rather than evaluative. They ask about people rather than performance. They leave encouraged rather than diminished because they never turned the evening into an audit of their own adequacy.

The less happy version of the reunion is the drive home afterward. You begin with one comparison and then, because the mind is efficient when misused, it starts assembling a larger case. His career progressed faster. Her children seem more settled. They travel more. Their house is probably nicer. Their retirement appears more secure. By the time you pull into your own driveway, you have used other people's visible facts to prosecute your own life.

None of this produces wisdom. It produces agitation.

The Curated Life

The digital age did not invent comparison, but it industrialized it. There has never been another time in human history when people were exposed to so many polished glimpses of other people's lives in such a concentrated and continuous form. Vacations, renovations, anniversaries, promotions, smiling family photographs, children receiving awards, meals photographed at flattering angles, achievements posted with just enough modesty to remain socially acceptable, and just enough visibility to do what they were actually posted to do.

To be clear, I am not arguing that people should never share good news. Joy ought to be shared. Gratitude ought to be expressed. But if you consume a steady diet of other people's highlights without remembering what they are, you will begin to treat your own ordinary Tuesday as evidence that something has gone wrong.

What has gone wrong is not your life. It is the frame.

There is also a quieter form of comparison that happens among people who care deeply about doing the right thing. Parents compare their parenting. Leaders compare their influence. Couples compare the apparent ease of other marriages to the actual work of their own. People compare their spiritual lives, their discipline, their houses, their vacations, their waistlines, their retirement accounts, and then wonder why contentment feels out of reach.

It feels out of reach because comparison moves the goalposts every time you get near them.

What Comparison Gets Wrong

Comparison assumes that the good in another person's life has some bearing on the value of yours. It does not. Their success is not your failure. Their beauty is not your deficiency. Their season is not your sentence. Most of the misery comparison comes from treating someone else's chapter as commentary on yours.

That is not how chapters work.

I have known people with modest means and deep peace. I have known people with every visible marker of success who could not rest in any room they entered. The difference was rarely external. It was interpretive. One group used life as something to be inhabited. The other used it as a competition to be monitored.

The cure for comparison is not pretending to notice anyone else. It is learning how to notice without measuring. Admire without ranking. Appreciate without converting another person's strength into evidence against yourself. Be genuinely glad for what is good in their life while remaining responsible for building a life that actually fits your values.

The more specific your values become, the weaker comparison becomes. Millard, whose story arrives later in this book, had an unusual immunity to comparison because he had decided very early what mattered to him and built accordingly. Once a person knows what a good life means to them, the spectacle of other people's lives loses much of its coercive force.

A Practical Exchange

If comparison has been stealing joy from you, try a simple exchange. The next time you feel the sideways pull, stop and ask: What exactly am I comparing right now? Name it specifically.

Then ask a second question: is that actually one of my values, or is it simply one of the culture's values that I borrowed without examination? That second question is often the entire breakthrough.

Many people are exhausted chasing lives they do not actually want.

The goal is not to think less of other people. It is to stop thinking of yourself through the wrong lens. Happiness grows when the measuring instrument changes from relative status to faithful stewardship. Am I living my life well? Am I present with the people I love? Am I doing work that matters? Am I grateful for what is here? Am I becoming the kind of person I would respect if no one were watching?

Those questions do not eliminate ambition. They purify it.

There is a final thing worth saying here. Comparison is not only a thief of joy, it is also a thief of courage. People who are constantly measuring themselves against others become less willing to attempt the thing that is actually theirs to do. They hesitate, second-guess, and shrink. The antidote is not self-esteem. It is clarity. Know the assignment that belongs to your life and then give yourself to it. That is enough work for any one person.

The happiest lives I know are not the most impressive from a distance. They are the most inhabited from within.

The Promotion Board

There is a particular kind of comparison that arrives not when someone else has something you want, but when someone else has something you believe you deserved equally. The neighbor's new car is easy to dismiss. The colleague who got the promotion you were also considered for is considerably harder.

The gap between those two experiences is the gap between envy and injustice, and it is a gap that comparison will gladly collapse for you if you let it.

I watched this happen in the Navy for years, and I watched it with a particular clarity because I was close enough to understand the mechanics and honest enough to understand what the mechanics actually meant.

When I graduated from the United States Naval Academy and entered the nuclear submarine service, my promotion path through the junior and mid-grade officer ranks was, by the standards of the broader Navy, unusually clear. Nuclear power required an extraordinary amount of training and qualification, which meant the pipeline was smaller and the competition for billets was genuine but manageable. My promotions came on time or early. I did not spend much energy thinking about the process because the process was, for me, working.

That changed as my contemporaries and I approached the senior ranks.

The transition to O-6, Navy Captain, and beyond into the four Admiral ranks is where the Navy's promotion system becomes something fundamentally different from what preceded it. Below that threshold, the question the promotion board is essentially asking is: Did this officer meet the standard? The answer is usually yes or no, and the standard is clear enough that most qualified people make it through.

At the senior ranks, the question changes. It becomes: of all the officers who met the standard, which ones do we have room for? The answer to that question is not determined by performance alone, because at that level, nearly everyone's performance is extraordinary by ordinary measures. The resumes are all remarkable. The sacrifices are all real. The families that moved every three years, the deployments, the assignments chosen specifically because they were difficult and qualification-building rather than comfortable, these things are present in almost every file that reaches a senior promotion board.

And yet a significant number of those officers will not be promoted.

I attended social events during those years, the kind of gatherings that military communities produce with regularity, and I listened to the conversations that happened in the corners of those rooms when someone had just been passed over. I heard officers say, with genuine conviction, that they deserved to be promoted over the people who had been selected. I heard spouses who had moved their families every three years say that the sacrifice had been made in exchange for something, and that something had not materialized, and that the people who had been selected were not meaningfully better than the people who had not.

The arguments were reasonable on their face. I took the challenging assignments. My performance exceeded that of my peers. The board did not know what I gave up to be here. I understood the feelings. I did not, on reflection, entirely agree with the analysis.

Here is what I came to believe about senior military promotions, having watched them from close enough range to have some perspective: at that level, the differences between candidates are genuinely small. Not negligible, but small. Everyone who reaches a senior promotion board has a significant resume, or they would not have reached it. The competition is not between the qualified and the unqualified. It is between the qualified and the slightly more fortunate.

By fortune, I mean several things simultaneously. Being in the right assignment at the right moment when something extraordinary happened, and therefore having an extraordinary performance on record. Being known, in the particular way that senior military communities are small enough to produce genuine personal familiarity, to someone sitting on the board. Having a set of experiences that happened to match what the service needed in its senior ranks at that particular moment in history is a function of timing as much as anything else.

I left the Navy after my O-6 promotion, which meant I did not experience the Admiral selection process directly. But three of my close friends did make Admiral, and they communicated to me, in various ways over the years, something I found illuminating: one of them would likely have served on my promotion board for Admiral. He was not suggesting this as a guarantee. He was noting it as a reality of how the system worked at that level. The people who know you and respect your work are not going to fabricate a record for you. But when a board is choosing among candidates whose differences are genuinely small, being known to someone in that room is worthwhile.

I retired before I had the chance to find out whether it would have made the difference.

Lesson

The officers and spouses who were angry in those corner conversations were not wrong to feel what they felt. The sacrifice was real. The performance was real. The conviction that they had done what was asked of them and earned what they were expecting was entirely understandable.

What comparison was doing to them, in those conversations, was turning a small difference into a verdict. It was taking the gap between their outcome and someone else's outcome and reading that gap as evidence about their worth, their service, their value as officers and human beings. It was using someone else's promotion as commentary on their career.

That is not what the promotion board's decision meant. The board was not saying that the passed-over officer was inadequate. It was saying that the selected officer was marginally better positioned, by a combination of performance, timing, familiarity, and the particular needs of the service at that moment, for the available slots.

The distinction matters because the first reading produces bitterness, and bitterness has a long shelf life in careers and in lives. The officers who read the non-selection as a verdict spent years carrying it. The officers who understood it as one moment in a system with genuine constraints and then redirected their energy toward what was still available to them, tended to find that what was still available to them was quite a lot.

One of the most useful questions to ask in any situation where comparison is generating pain is: what exactly is being compared, and what does that comparison actually mean? In the case of a senior military promotion board, what is being compared is a set of extraordinary resumes in a system that has room for a fraction of the people who deserve advancement. The person selected is not better than the person passed over in any meaningful sense of the word better. They are the person the system had room for at that moment.

That is important. But it is also not a verdict.

The sun came up the morning after every one of those promotion announcements. For some people, it rose on a new rank. For others, it rose on a career that still had decades of significant contribution ahead of it, if they were willing to stop measuring themselves against a board's decision and start investing in what the day was actually offering.

The ones who made that choice are, in my opinion, the happier ones.

Chapter 3

THE WORRY TRAP

Worry has excellent marketing. It presents itself as responsibility, as love, as the price of caring deeply about something. The person who worries, the story goes, is the person who takes things seriously. The person who does not worry is naive, careless, dangerously optimistic about a world that does not reward optimism.

This is one of the most effective lies the mind tells itself. Worry is not a form of preparation. It is a form of suffering that arrives before the thing it is supposedly preparing for, and that, most of the time, prepares you for nothing because the thing never happens. The worry was all cost and no benefit. And then the next worry boards.

Humans worry because they believe worry protects them. If we imagine the bad outcome clearly enough, the thinking goes, perhaps we can prevent it, or at least be prepared for it when it arrives. Worry feels like diligence. It feels like caring. It feels like the responsible thing to do.

It is almost never any of those things.

Research consistently shows that the vast majority of what we worry about never happens. And for the small fraction that does materialize, the worry that preceded it rarely made us more prepared. It makes us tired, anxious, and less present in the life that was actually happening while we were rehearsing the one we feared.

This is particularly true of parents, who invest so much of their emotional lives in their children that the worry seems inseparable from the love. It is not. They are different things. The love is essential. The worry, most of the time, is a tax on joy. Karen's story makes the case more clearly than any statistic could.

The 11-Minute Window

Karen's son had been gone for eleven minutes.

He was eleven years old, riding his bike to his friend Dillon's house, four blocks away, a route he'd ridden forty times. She knew this. And yet.

Minute two: She checked her phone. No text. Normal. He never texted.

Minute four: She moved to the window. The street was quiet. Too quiet, she thought, which was insane because she'd also complained for years that the street was too loud.

Minute six: A full cinematic sequence had begun in her mind, the distracted driver, the unfamiliar dog, the patch of wet leaves on the corner of Elm. She had called the paramedics. She had chosen the hospital. She had, God help her, begun mentally composing what she would say to Dillon's mother.

Minute eight: She texted her husband: "Has Tyler checked in with you?" He replied: "He left 8 minutes ago, Karen." She typed back: "I know that."

Minute nine: She was now certain, not worried, certain, that something was wrong. The silence had a texture. Mothers know things. This was a thing she knew.

Minute eleven: The garage door rumbled. Bike tires on concrete. Tyler's voice: "MOM. Have you seen my other cleat? Dillon wants to kick the ball around."

He had never made it to Dillon's house. He had turned around, of his own free eleven-year-old will, to retrieve a shoe. Karen stood in the kitchen for a moment, her disaster narrative still warm in her hands like a prop from a play that had just been cancelled.

"It's in the mudroom," she said.

"Thanks." He grabbed it and was gone again.

She poured herself a glass of water and looked out the window at the perfectly ordinary street. The catastrophe had been cancelled. The next one was already boarding.

Lesson

The Worry Trap isn't solved by things going right. It just reloads. That is what makes it a trap.

The comedy of the eleven-minute window is the point of entry. But the real insight is in that last image. Karen's son came home safely, and rather than feeling relief and returning to her day, she was already generating the next scenario. The worry machine doesn't stop when the danger passes. It recalibrates and looks for something new to process.

The antidote is not positive thinking. It is the disciplined practice of distinguishing between what is actually happening and what we are imagining might happen. Most of the time, the street outside is perfectly ordinary. Most of the time, the catastrophe is already boarding a different flight entirely.

The Tracking App

Sandra had the app installed before Connor started kindergarten.

It was reasonable at the time. He was five. The school was three miles away. The app showed a small blue dot moving along a map, and the small blue dot was her son, and knowing where the small blue dot was at all times seemed like exactly the kind of thing a responsible parent did in the current era. She mentioned it to her husband, Phil, who nodded in the way that he nodded when he had learned that some conversations were not actually invitations for his opinion.

The app stayed on Connor's phone when he was eight. And ten. And twelve, when he started riding his bike to a friend's house, and Sandra watched the blue dot travel the four blocks in real time from her kitchen, setting down her coffee only after it had been stationary at the correct address for ninety seconds.

By the time Connor was fourteen, Sandra had developed what she privately thought of as a blue dot fluency. She could read the dot the way a sailor reads the weather. Speed of movement: was he running, which was fine, or sprinting, which meant something was wrong, or stationary for longer than expected, which meant something was either very wrong or he had stopped to talk to someone, which opened its own category of concerns. Location relative to expected location: was he where he said he would be, and if not, how far off course, and in which direction, and toward what?

Phil occasionally reminded her, gently, that Connor was fourteen.

Sandra occasionally agreed and then checked the app.

The conversation that changed things happened on a Sunday afternoon when Connor was fifteen and asked to go to the movies with three friends. Sandra said yes. She located the theater on the app, established the expected dot position, and was sitting in the living room with the app open when Phil sat down next to her.

He did not say anything for a moment. He looked at the phone. He looked at her.

"What would happen," he said, "if you didn't know where he was right now?"

Sandra looked up. "What do you mean?"

"I mean, what would happen. Specifically. What would actually happen?"

She thought about it. Connor was at the movies. The theater was in a mall. The mall was in a suburb that had been safe for thirty years. His friends were boys she had known since second grade. He had his phone. He was fifteen years old and six feet tall.

"I would worry," she said.

"And then what?"

She didn't answer immediately.

"Nothing," she said finally. "Nothing would happen. He'd come home."

Phil nodded. He did not press further. He learned, over fifteen years of marriage, that the right question asked once and then left alone did more work than the same question asked repeatedly.

Sandra looked at the blue dot. It was stationary inside the theater, which was exactly where it was supposed to be, and she was sitting in her living room watching it instead of reading the book that had been on her nightstand since March.

She put the phone face-down on the cushion beside her.

She picked up the book.

She lasted eleven minutes before she picked the phone back up. But the eleven minutes were something. They were, she would say later, the beginning of something.

The thing Sandra came to understand, slowly and over the following year in a way that Phil had the good grace never to mention he saw coming, was that the app was not really about Connor's safety. Connor was, by any reasonable assessment, fine. He was a healthy, reasonably responsible teenager doing teenager things in a reasonably safe environment, and the probability that any of her watching ever prevented any harm to him was essentially zero.

The app was about her anxiety. And her anxiety, she gradually admitted, was not really about Connor either. It was about the unbearable vulnerability of loving someone that much and having no control over what happened to them.

That was the real thing underneath the blue dot. The love was so large and the helplessness so total that the only thing that made it bearable was the illusion of information. If she knew where he was, she felt like she was doing something. She felt like the love was being expressed in a concrete, protective form rather than just sitting inside her, enormous and unmanageable, and pointed at a person who was growing, quite naturally, away from her.

The problem was that Connor knew she was watching. Of course, he knew. He was fifteen, not five. And what the watching communicated to him, beneath all the genuine love that motivated it, was a message Sandra never intended to send: I don't trust you to be okay without me tracking you.

She had a conversation with him about it one evening, which was one of the hardest conversations of her parenting life, not because Connor was angry, he wasn't, particularly, but because of something he said near the end of it that she has thought about many times since.

"Mom," he said, "I'm not going to do anything bad. But even if I were going to, the dot wouldn't stop me. It would just mean you'd find out faster."

She stared at him.

"You're right," she said.

"I know," he said, with the serene confidence of a fifteen-year-old who has just won an argument with a parent and is being careful not to celebrate.

Sandra deleted the app three days later; not in a single heroic act of trust, but after two more days of checking it and feeling, each time, the specific low-grade shame of someone caught doing something they know is slightly ridiculous. The shame finally outweighed the comfort.

Connor came home from school that afternoon, and she told him.

He shrugged in the way that teenagers shrug when they are pleased but unwilling to make a production of it.

"Cool," he said, and went to his room.

She stood in the kitchen for a moment and noticed that she did not, in fact, know where he was. He was somewhere in the house, presumably his room, and she had not confirmed this with technology, and nothing about that uncertainty felt as terrible as she expected it to.

It felt, she realized, approximately like what parenting probably felt like before there were apps. Which was to say, it felt like love without a security blanket. Warmer than she remembered.

Phil came home an hour later, saw her reading on the couch, and asked how her day was.

"Fine," she said. "Good, actually."

He noticed the phone was on the cushion beside her, face-up, with no app open. He did not say anything. He went to the kitchen and started dinner. He learned, over fifteen years, that some victories were best appreciated quietly.

The story Sandra tells now, when other parents of teenagers bring up the tracking app conversation, and they always bring it up, because every parent of a teenager in the current era has had some version of this conversation with themselves, is not that the app was wrong. She is careful about that. For a five-year-old, the app made sense. For a twelve-year-old in a genuinely uncertain situation, it might make sense. The tool is not the problem.

The question she asks now is the one Phil asked on that Sunday afternoon: what would actually happen if you didn't know?

For most parents, most of the time, the honest answer is the same one Sandra arrived at. Nothing. The child would come home. The worry would have been real, and the outcome would have been fine, and the watching would not have been the reason.

What the watching costs, and this is what Sandra did not account for when she installed the app before kindergarten, is the message it sends. Not the message you intend, which is I love you and want you to be safe. The message the child receives, accumulated over years of being tracked through adolescence: I am not sure you can handle this without me watching.

That message, delivered consistently enough, tends to become a belief. And a child who believes they cannot handle things without someone watching them grows into an adult who is not entirely sure they can handle things alone.

Sandra did not want to raise that adult. She wanted to raise Connor, who was already, at fifteen, more capable than the app had ever given him credit for.

The blue dot had been showing her his location for a decade. It had never once shown her who he was becoming.

Chapter 4

THE MORNING WE CHOOSE

We make thousands of decisions every day, most of them without noticing. What to eat? Which route to take? How to respond to an email? Whether to read the news. These decisions accumulate into something larger than any individual choice: they become the texture of how we experience our days, and eventually, our lives.

The decisions we make in the first hour of the morning are disproportionately powerful. This is not motivational speculation. It reflects something real about how the brain works: the mood, mindset, and emotional tone established early in the day create a lens through which everything that follows is interpreted. Start the day in a state of anxiety and low-grade alarm, and ordinary events look like confirmation of something threatening. Start it grounded and oriented toward what is good, and the same events look manageable, sometimes even interesting.

We have more control over this than most people exercise. The morning is not neutral ground. It is where the day is won or lost before it begins.

The Morning Diet

Situation

Years ago, I heard a motivational speaker say something that stuck with me and eventually changed how I start every day. He said most people wake up, get dressed, make breakfast, and do it all with the local news running in the background. And what does the local news give you?

Traffic. A major crash on the Dallas side of the metroplex, expect two-hour delays. Weather. A snowstorm hammering the Rockies, people losing power. Crime. Murders in the city. Neighbors taking advantage of neighbors.

He paused and said: “Next time you watch the news, count how much of it is positive.”

His point wasn’t really about the news. It was about the mood you carry into your day. You haven’t even poured your second cup of coffee and you’re already anxious, already braced, already a little beaten down. You started the day in a hole you didn’t dig.

His recommendation was simple: turn it off. Replace it with something that puts you in the right frame of mind, reflection, an inspiring book, something that expands your thinking rather than contracts it.

Turning Point

I decided to test his theory first. The next morning, I watched the news and kept score. Not the 75% negative he had suggested. A solid 90%. That was enough for me.

I turned it off. That was many years ago, and I have not looked back.

Do I sometimes show up dressed for the wrong weather? Yes. Do I hit traffic jams I didn’t see coming? Of course. I genuinely cannot tell you which channel carries which network anymore.

But I can tell you this: I live a happier life. And it started with what I chose to let in before 8 a.m.

Lesson

What we feed our minds early in the day shapes how we experience everything that follows. The morning is not neutral ground. It is where the day is won or lost before it begins.

This does not require a morning routine of elaborate complexity. It requires one decision: what is the first thing I choose to let in? The answer to that question, made consistently over time, shapes more of a life than most people realize.

The Forecast She Didn't Check

Situation

Margaret checked the weather every morning for thirty-one years.

Not glanced at it. Checked it. The full report: current temperature, feels-like temperature, hourly breakdown, precipitation probability by the hour, extended forecast, and, after the apps became sophisticated enough to offer it, the UV index, the air quality rating, and something called the comfort level, which Margaret never fully understood but checked anyway on the theory that more information was always better than less.

She was a high school principal. She had two children, a husband who traveled for work three weeks out of four, a commute that involved a highway that flooded in heavy rain, and a campus that required someone to make decisions about outdoor activities, field trips, and dismissal procedures. The weather, she would have told you, was professionally relevant.

This was true. It was also, she came to understand much later, not the real reason.

The real reason was that the weather check was the first act of control she performed each day. Before anything else could be uncertain, before the emails arrived, before the schedule asserted itself, before the particular chaos of running a school of twelve hundred students revealed whatever it had prepared for her that morning, she knew the weather. She had that. It was a small, concrete piece of the day she could hold in her hand before the rest of it was handed to her.

She did not know this about herself for a long time. She thought she was just checking the weather.

The morning that reframed everything was a Tuesday in October, the kind of morning that arrives without fanfare and turns out to matter.

Turning Point

Her phone died overnight. She forgot to plug it in, which happened perhaps twice a year and which she always treated as a minor emergency requiring immediate correction. On this particular morning, however, she was running late, the kind of late that announces itself at the moment you open your eyes and does not relent, and she made the decision, consciously and with some reluctance, to leave the dead phone on the nightstand and go.

She drove to work without the weather report.

The sky, visible through the windshield, looked like October. Cool. Partly cloudy. A reasonable day by any visible assessment. But she had no data. She had no percentage. She had no hourly breakdown telling her whether the clouds would clear by noon or thicken by three. She had only the sky, which was doing what the sky does, which is to say it was simply there, offering no predictions and making no promises.

She noticed, somewhere on the highway, that she felt slightly untethered. Not anxious exactly. Lighter than usual, but in a way that took a moment to name. As if something she normally carried had been left on the nightstand with the phone.

The day proceeded. She wore a jacket that turned out to be appropriate. The clouds cleared by mid-morning. It did not rain. The outdoor event scheduled for the afternoon happened without incident.

Not a single thing about the day required the weather report she had not checked.

She sat in her office at the end of the afternoon, which had been a perfectly ordinary Tuesday with the usual assortment of problems and small victories, and thought about what had been different. Something had been different. She turned it over until she found it.

She had not started the day braced.

This required some examination.

Margaret was not, by temperament, an anxious person. She was decisive, organized, professionally confident, the kind of leader people described as unflappable in a crisis. But she had, without ever articulating it to herself, developed a morning ritual that was quietly oriented toward potential threat. The weather check was the first item, but it was not the only one. There was also the school's email inbox, which she checked before leaving the house, and which occasionally contained something that required immediate attention, more often contained something that would require eventual attention and almost always contained something that made her begin the drive already thinking about a problem.

There was also the local news, which she had on in the background while she got ready, and which offered the usual inventory: traffic delays, overnight incidents, weather warnings, and the particular selection of stories that local news favors, which are the ones most likely to produce a state of low-grade alarm in a person who is only half listening while putting on shoes.

She had never thought of any of these as choices. They were simply what mornings were. The information was there, and she consumed it, and then she drove to work carrying it.

The Tuesday without the phone had shown her, for the first time, what the morning felt like without it.

It felt like she had arrived at work with more of herself intact.

She did not throw away her phone, cancel the weather app, or stop reading email before she left the house. She was a principal with genuine professional responsibilities, and some of the morning information consumption was legitimately necessary. But she started making distinctions she had not made before.

The highway traffic report: genuinely useful. She adjusted her departure time based on it, and it saved her real minutes.

The weather check: useful as a quick glance, unnecessary as a thirty-minute investigation of comfort levels and UV indices for a woman who was going to be inside a building for most of the day.

The news in the background: not useful. Not even, on reflection, informative in any way that shaped her day constructively. What it reliably produced was a mild, ambient awareness of things that were going wrong somewhere that she could not influence in any way, delivered at the precise moment when she was forming her initial relationship with the day.

She started turning it off.

Not forever. Not as a philosophical position. Just in the morning, for the forty minutes between waking and leaving, which she began treating as a kind of protected time, protected not from information in general but from information that arrived in a frame of alarm and left without resolution.

She replaced it, initially somewhat self-consciously, with quiet. Then, with a podcast she genuinely enjoyed. Then, with music she had not listened to in years because the news had been on instead. Then, on the mornings when she woke early enough, with coffee and twenty minutes of reading something that had nothing to do with school administration or current events or anything she was responsible for.

The school did not suffer. The students did not suffer. The problems that required her attention each day continued to present themselves at exactly the same rate as before, entirely indifferent to whether she had heard about them in advance.

What changed was how she arrived.

Her assistant, a woman named Carol who had worked with three principals before Margaret and had developed a fine-grained sensitivity to the emotional weather of school leadership, noticed the difference before Margaret mentioned it.

"You seem different in the mornings," Carol said one day. Not a question. An observation offered carefully, the way Carol offered most things.

"Different how?" Margaret asked.

Carol thought about it. "Like you got here without carrying anything yet."

Margaret considered that for a moment.

"That's exactly what it is," she said.

Lesson

What Margaret discovered, through the accidental experiment of a dead phone and a Tuesday in October, is something she now describes as the difference between being informed and being primed.

Being informed means knowing what you need to know in order to do your job and move through your day. It is useful, necessary, and worth attending to.

Being primed means arriving at your day already tuned to a particular frequency, usually one of mild vigilance, low-grade concern, or the background hum of things-that-are-wrong-in-the-world, before the day has had a chance to be anything at all.

Most morning information consumption, she came to believe, is priming rather than informing. The news is not telling you things you need in order to act. It is tuning your nervous system to a particular register before you walk out the door. And that register, carried into the first meeting and the first conversation and the first decision of the day, shapes everything that follows in ways that are almost invisible precisely because they feel like simply how you feel.

Margaret still checks the weather. A glance, now. Enough to know whether to bring an umbrella. Not enough to develop an opinion about the comfort level. She arrives at school most mornings feeling, as Carol put it, as if she hadn't carried anything yet.

The day always brings plenty to carry. She has found it is better to pick it up there, where it actually is, than to collect it in advance from a screen and haul it through the front door before the first bell rings. The sky does what the sky does. It has never once asked her permission. She stopped, mostly, trying to prepare for it in advance.

It is still there every morning through the windshield, offering no predictions and making no promises, and she came to find this genuinely, surprisingly, okay.

Chapter 5

MONEY, ENOUGH, AND CONTENTMENT

Money matters. Anyone who says otherwise has either forgotten what financial stress feels like or never felt it in the first place. Money pays the rent, buys groceries, keeps the lights on, and creates options when life turns unexpectedly difficult. It can relieve pressure, preserve dignity, and protect the people we love from burdens they should not have to carry alone.

But money is not the same thing as contentment. I spent most of my professional life helping people make financial decisions, and one of the most consistent things I observed was that peace does not rise in direct proportion to net worth. Some people with very little slept well. Some people with a great deal did not. Some were prudent without being consumed. Others were secure on paper and still lived as if catastrophe were standing just outside the door.

The question, then, is not whether money matters. It does. The better question is: what money is for?

At its best, money does more than buy things. It relieves fear, creates options, protects dignity, and sometimes becomes one of the clearest ways love is made visible. I learned that lesson not in an office, but across a dinner table from my daughter.

The Statement

I learned something as a financial advisor that sounds, on the surface, like a mathematical observation: small amounts of money, set aside consistently over time, accumulate into something larger than most people expect. Compound interest is the technical term. What it actually is, when you watch it arrive in someone's life at exactly the right moment, is something the technical term does not capture at all.

This is a story about that. But it is not really a story about money.

Situation

Our daughter was always a good one.

I do not say that the way parents say it when they are being politely general about a child they love. I mean it as a specific and accurate description. She moved through her years with a decency and a thoughtfulness that made the parenting feel, more often than not, like the privilege it actually was.

What also happened, as it often happens with daughters and their mothers, is that the closeness between her and my wife went through a renegotiation during the high school years. Not a rupture. A renegotiation. For most of her childhood, her best friend had been her mother. Then her body changed, her world expanded, and the person she had once been most open with became, for a season, the person she was most guarded with. This is not unusual. It is one of the most common and most quietly painful transitions in family life. My wife handled it with more grace than I would have managed in her position.

I had an idea.

I asked my wife whether she would let me take our daughter out on dates, just the two of us. Not because I wanted to exclude her; anyone who knows how much my wife enjoys a good dinner out will understand what I was really asking; but because I sensed our daughter needed a place where she could talk without worrying about anyone's reaction. To her credit, my wife said yes.

Those date nights became something I looked forward to far more than I expected.

She talked about school, friends, and the particular interior weather of being a teenage girl trying to make sense of a changing world. I will be honest: the specific content was not always something I would have chosen to spend an evening on. But I listened. And I mean I actually listened, the way you listen when you understand that the subject matter is secondary and the listening itself is the point. I offered thoughts from time to time. Mostly I listened.

What I received in return was my daughter's trust, which is not a small thing and which I did not take for granted.

Turning Point

As her senior year unfolded and graduation approached, I decided our final date night before college would be different. I made a reservation at a private club. I told her to dress for the occasion. We were celebrating both her birthday and her graduation, and the evening deserved to be marked accordingly.

The staff knew it was special. A rose was presented on a velvet pillow. The room was warm. The dinner was excellent. Sitting across from me was a young woman I was deeply proud of in a way I had not yet fully said out loud.

We talked about the years. She was reflective in a way that surprised me with its depth. She talked about what our support had meant to her, about things she had noticed that she had never really thanked us for, about what she was carrying into the next chapter and what she was grateful to be carrying. I told her I was going to miss her when she left for college in the fall. It was true, and I had not fully let myself feel it until I said it.

Then I told her there was something I wanted to show her. Something she did not know.

Since she was young, I had been putting money away for her. Not large amounts. Regular amounts, set aside each month, quietly and consistently over the years. I had done the same for each of our children, and later for our grandchildren. It never felt like a sacrifice. It felt like a commitment made once and then honored over time.

I pulled out the statement.

She looked at the number. She looked at me. Then she asked whether that was the real amount; not a projection, not a someday number, but the actual amount sitting in an account with her name on it.

I told her it was.

Our daughter began to cry. Not the polite kind of tears that appear at sentimental moments and are quickly managed. The real kind. The kind that come from somewhere deep and arrive before the person has made any decision about whether to let them.

She told me it was one of the best days of her life. She said she had been carrying, quietly and without telling us, an anxiety about how college would be paid for. And the number on that statement meant she could go without that burden. She could simply go.

I did not say much after that. There was not much to say. The statement had said the thing, and her tears had received it, and we sat together in that dining room for a few moments in the particular silence of a moment that needs nothing added to it.

Lesson

I have thought about that evening many times since, and about what it clarified for me regarding something I had long said to clients but had not fully felt until I watched it happen across a dinner table. Investing money is not, at its core, an analytical activity. The analysis is the vehicle. The destination is emotional.

The spreadsheet does not matter very much. The compound interest calculation does not matter very much. The monthly contribution amount, the rate of return, the years in the account; those things matter only because they produce the thing that actually matters: the moment when the accumulation of small, patient, consistent decisions becomes visible to the person it was made for.

My daughter did not cry because of the interest rate. She cried because someone had been thinking about her future, quietly and without announcement, for years before the future arrived. The money was simply the evidence of that. It was proof, in a form she could hold in her hands, that her path had been prepared for, that she was not walking into the next chapter alone, that the love present throughout her childhood had also been present in a savings account, adding a little each month, waiting for her.

That is what money can do when it is used correctly. Not as an end. Not as a measure of status. Not as a scoreboard. But as a concrete expression of care, accumulated over time and delivered at the moment it is needed most.

Financial independence is not a number. It is a feeling. And when that feeling arrives, it sometimes looks exactly like the tears of a young woman who just learned that someone loved her carefully enough to prepare the road before she knew she would need to walk it.

A Note on the Story Behind the Story

The date nights themselves deserve mention separate from the graduation dinner, because they carry their own lesson.

The decision to take your daughter out alone, to ask your wife to step aside so the space could become what it needed to be, to sit across from a teenager talking about things that did not particularly interest you and listen anyway; that is not a financial story. It is a story about relationships. It is the story of a father who understood that presence is not passive, that listening is active, and that the trust of a teenage daughter is not automatically given to a parent who loves her.

It is given to the parent who shows up in the way the daughter needs, not in the way that is most comfortable for the parent.

The statement at the end of the graduation dinner was the financial chapter. The date nights were the relational foundation that made the statement mean what it did. Without them, the gift would have been generous. With them, it became something more. It became the closing of a chapter that had been written one dinner at a time across the years of her growing up.

That is, in the end, what this whole book is about: the small, consistent, intentional investments; in money, in time, in attention, in presence; that accumulate into something larger than any single contribution could produce. The sun came up every morning of those high school years. Most of them were ordinary. All of them were adding up to something.

What Money is For

Money will never remove all uncertainty. It was not designed to do that. But it can do something noble when it is handled wisely and held with the right spirit. It can turn love into preparedness. It can relieve pressure before pressure becomes panic. It can make it possible for someone you care about to step into the future with a little more freedom and a little less fear.

That, to me, is what contentment has always meant in financial life. Not extravagance. Not endless accumulation. Not proving anything. Contentment is the quiet steadiness that comes from knowing what is enough, preparing for what matters, and refusing to let money become more important than the people it is meant to serve.

I have known people with very little who lived with that steadiness, and I have known people with every visible sign of success who did not. Enough is partly a number, of course. Bills do not pay themselves. But after a certain point, enough becomes a way of seeing. It becomes the difference between using money as a tool and letting it become a verdict on your worth.

When money is used well, it does not enlarge ego. It enlarges options, generosity, and peace. It helps prepare the road for the people we love. And when it does that, it becomes one more way of living the central truth of this book: small, steady acts of care add up. Sometimes they add up to a conversation. Sometimes they add up to trust. And sometimes they add up to tears at a dinner table when a young woman discovers that love has been quietly compounding for years.

Compound interest is the technical term. But when you watch it arrive in someone's life at exactly the right moment, you realize the technical term does not capture what is really happening at all.

Chapter 6

FAITH, TRUST, AND SURRENDER

There are some things in life we can prepare for and some we cannot. Wisdom teaches us to know the difference. Faith teaches us how to live with what remains uncertain.

The Waiting Room

Situation

Thomas Garrett had solved most of the problems he had ever faced. This was not arrogance. It was simply true.

He had built a business from nothing over twenty-two years. He survived a market collapse that took out three competitors and kept his company standing. He raised two sons largely alone after his wife left when the boys were seven and four, and he had done it well enough that both of them became, by any honest measure, good men.

When problems came, Thomas handled them. He did not know what to do with a problem he could not handle. The diagnosis came on a Tuesday in November, which is the kind of detail that lodges permanently in memory whether you want it to or not.

Pancreatic cancer. Stage three.

The oncologist was direct, compassionate, and experienced in delivering news no one wants to hear. She outlined the treatment plan. She used words like 'aggressive' and 'challenging,' and "we will do everything we can."

Thomas heard the words with the part of his mind that processed language. He did not yet feel them with the part that processed reality. He drove home. He sat in his car in the garage for eleven minutes without going inside. He was trying to locate, among all the resources that had served him for sixty-one years, the one that applied to this.

He could not find it.

Treatment began three weeks later. Chemotherapy, then radiation, then a surgical evaluation to determine whether the tumor responded enough to make surgery possible. The timeline stretched across months. The outcome was genuinely uncertain. Thomas respected his doctor's honesty and, at intervals, found it nearly unbearable.

He was not a man who paid close attention to his faith for most of his adult life. He grew up in a home where church was regular, and God was assumed, and he carried that assumption into adulthood the way people carry the furniture of childhood, present in the background, rarely examined.

He believed, approximately. He prayed occasionally, briefly, in the way of someone placing an order rather than beginning a conversation.

What he discovered after the diagnosis was that approximate faith is sufficient for approximate circumstances and genuinely insufficient for the ones that are not approximate at all. He needed something more than he had been maintaining.

There was a man at his church named Walter, a retired schoolteacher in his seventies who survived his own cancer diagnosis eleven years earlier. Walter had the kind of presence some people acquire only after standing at the edge of something and returning without pretending the edge was not there. Thomas had known him for years in the way people know each other at church, friendly, sincere, but not close.

Turning Point

He called Walter on a Thursday evening in December. The call surprised both of them. Thomas did not entirely know why he called. He only knew that Walter had been through something and had come through it looking like a man who had made peace with the terms of his life.

That was what Thomas wanted. Not information. Not a strategy. Peace. Walter listened without interrupting, which was the first thing Thomas noticed. Then he asked, "Tell me what you are trying to control."

"The outcome," Thomas said.

Walter was quiet for a moment.

"You cannot control the outcome," he said. "You already know that. That's why you called me instead of your doctor. The real question is what you do with the part of you that keeps trying anyway."

Thomas said, "I don't know how to stop trying."

Walter said, "You do not stop trying. You keep doing everything the doctors tell you to do. Every treatment. Every protocol. Every instruction. You show up fully for the part that is yours to do. And then you put the outcome somewhere else. You give it to something larger than yourself and leave it there. And when you find yourself reaching for it again in the middle of the night, which you will, you put it back."

Thomas said, "That sounds simple."

Walter smiled. "It is simple. Simple is not the same as easy. I put the outcome back about four hundred times in the first month. It gets easier."

Thomas began going to church differently. Not more often, at least not at first. Differently. With the attention of someone who discovered that what he had been treating as decorative was actually structural.

He prayed differently, too. Not the order-placing kind. The conversational kind. It felt awkward at first, then gradually more natural than many things he had done in years. He was not certain of the theology. He did not resolve all the honest questions people have about prayer, whether it changes outcomes or only the person doing the praying. He held those questions and prayed anyway.

What changed was not his certainty. What changed was his posture. At first, he prayed the way frightened people often pray, please let this be okay. But that kind of prayer left him monitoring the world anxiously, looking for signs that the request was working.

What finally brought him peace was something different. It was the daily practice of putting the outcome down. Deliberately. Repeatedly.

Acknowledging that the outcome was not his to carry, that carrying it produced nothing useful and consumed everything he had, and then releasing it, not once and permanently, but daily and sometimes hourly, into something he trusted more than his own ability to manage it.

He was not always successful. Walter told him he would not be. But the practice changed his relationship to the waiting. The waiting room, once a place of concentrated dread, became somewhere he could sit without being completely consumed by what it represented.

He was still afraid. He did not stop being afraid. But the fear occupied a different amount of space than it had before he began putting the outcome down every morning. Six months after the diagnosis, the surgical evaluation came. The tumor had responded. The surgery was viable.

The surgeon was cautiously optimistic in the careful way surgeons are cautious, which Thomas learned to interpret accurately enough to know that this was genuinely good news. The operation took place on a Wednesday in May. His two sons sat in the waiting room for seven hours. The older one paced. The younger one sat still with his hands folded.

Thomas would later learn that this was how his son sat when he prayed. He had not known that about him. The knowledge moved him in a way he did not have words for.

The surgery was successful.

If you ask Thomas today what that season taught him, he will tell you he still does not know whether faith changed the medical outcome or only his experience of it. He holds that question honestly and without resolution. But he knows exactly what changed in him. He began that journey as a man who solved most of his problems and discovered that this one was not his to solve.

That discovery was disorienting. What Walter gave him was not reassurance, optimism, or a promise of a good ending. Walter gave him a practice. Do your part fully. Put the outcome down. Trust something larger with the rest.

Thomas knows the practice worked. Not as a guarantee. As a way of remaining present, functional, and genuinely alive during months that might otherwise have been consumed entirely by fear.

The younger version of Thomas would have called that surrender. The older version calls it something else.

He calls it the most useful thing he learned in sixty-one years. The thing waiting just beyond the edge of what effort can do. You do your part. Fully. Without reservation. Without using surrender as an excuse to stop showing up for what is yours to do. And then you put the outcome somewhere larger than yourself. You leave it there.

And when you reach for it again in the middle of the night, you put it back.

It gets easier.

Reflection

Faith does not always remove uncertainty. Trust does not always explain suffering. Surrender does not guarantee the outcome we want.

But they do something else.

They make it possible to keep living when life enters a season that cannot be controlled. There is peace in doing fully what is ours to do and releasing what is not.

Lesson

The deepest form of trust may be this: Do your part fully. Then put the outcome down. The sun still comes up, even when we are waiting for news we cannot control.

Part II

STOPS ALONG THE WAY

The moments and milestones that taught me what happiness actually is

A Note on Part II

The chapters that follow are drawn from my own life, though the lessons they carry belong to anyone who has worked a first job, welcomed a child, chased a dream, or found themselves redirected toward something they never planned for. I have included them not because my experiences are unusual, but because they are not. The stops along the way look different for everyone. The lessons they carry, I have found, are remarkably consistent.

Chapter 7

THE FIRST STOPS

The first stops are rarely glamorous. They are the places where we show up underprepared and overconfident, where the gap between who we think we are and who we actually are becomes visible for the first time. They are also, for exactly that reason, among the most instructive stops we ever make.

What we learn at the first stops tends to travel with us for the rest of the journey. The lesson about work that arrives before we know enough to appreciate it. The mentor who challenges us in ways we resent at the time and recall with gratitude for decades afterward. The failure that redirects us toward something we never would have chosen and cannot now imagine living without. These early lessons do not announce themselves as significant. They reveal their significance slowly, in hindsight, as the shape of a life becomes clear enough to read.

The earliest stops are where we learn what work actually is, what we are actually made of, and what our families were quietly teaching us all along. We rarely recognize any of this at the time. That is part of what makes those stops so instructive in hindsight.

The First Job Reality Check

There is a particular brand of confidence that belongs exclusively to teenagers who believe they are ready for the world. It is not arrogance exactly, though it resembles arrogance closely enough that adults often confuse the two. It is something closer to the genuine certainty of someone who has not yet been shown what they don't know. That certainty is useful, in its way. It makes young people willing to attempt things that older, wiser, more cautious people talk themselves out of.

It also makes them spectacular targets for the kind of lesson that can only be taught by reality.

Situation

The summer between my junior and senior year of high school, I decided I was ready for the real world. My father was president of a company, and I approached him about working there. In my mind, the job was already half-designed: a lab coat, some experiments, maybe a clipboard. The president's son, contributing something meaningful.

My father had a different idea.

He told me to apply like everyone else. He wasn't directly responsible for hiring summer help, and he wasn't going to make an exception. So, I filled out the application, turned it in, and waited.

I got the job. Just not the one I had in mind.

My assignment was maintenance, specifically, every task nobody else wanted. Mowing grass in the summer heat. Painting the exterior of the building in the full humidity of an Ohio summer. Breaking down metal framework inside warehouses with no air conditioning and decades of dust in the air.

No lab coat. No clipboard. Just work.

Turning Point

Somewhere between the third coat of exterior paint and another afternoon in a sweltering warehouse, something shifted. My father never lectured me. He never said "this is good for you" or "you need to understand how hard work feels." He didn't have to. The work said it for him.

I started doing the math on my own.

Lesson

My father taught me the value of education without ever once mentioning it. No speech. No warning. No pressure. Just a summer of honest, unglamorous labor that made the point more clearly than any conversation could have.

The lesson wasn't that hard work is bad. It's that preparation opens doors. The men I worked alongside that summer were doing necessary, dignified work. But I had a choice they may not have had. My father made sure I understood that choice, and what it would cost me if I took it for granted.

He was, quietly, one of the best teachers I ever had.

I have thought about that summer many times over the decades, usually when I am watching someone younger approach a situation with the same breezy confidence I had standing in my father's office with my imaginary lab coat. The instinct is always to tell them, to spare them the sweltering warehouse and the third coat of exterior paint. I learned to resist that instinct. Some lessons require the heat. The ones that arrive through lived experience tend to stay in ways that the ones delivered in a comfortable conversation almost never do.

My father understood something that I didn't articulate until I was a good deal older: the goal of parenting is not to protect your children from every hard thing. It is to arrange conditions where the right hard things find them at the right time, with enough support nearby that they don't break, but enough genuine difficulty that they grow. That summer was not punishment. It was curriculum. The lab coat I imagined wearing was not the education I needed. The paint brush was.

The Career Detour: Naval Academy

We make our plans with the information we have, which is never complete, and aim them at futures we can imagine, which are always narrower than what actually becomes possible. This is not a flaw in the planning. It is simply the nature of planning from inside a life that hasn't happened yet. The plans are not wrong. They are just drawn on a map that doesn't yet show all the roads.

Some of the best roads I have ever traveled were ones I only found because the road I intended to take was closed.

Situation

From the moment I arrived at the United States Naval Academy, I knew exactly where I was headed. Fighter pilot. Everything I did in those first two years pointed in that direction: the classmates I spent time with, the courses I selected, the future I rehearsed in my mind. I wanted speed, altitude, and the cockpit of the fastest aircraft the Navy could put me in.

Academically, I had done enough to qualify. There was only one obstacle left: the flight physical. And within that physical, one specific concern; the eye exam. I could see the 20/20 line. Most days. But there were moments when my eyes drifted out of focus, and on those days, that line disappeared. I knew the rule: uncorrected 20/20 vision, no exceptions.

I showed up to the exam and hoped it would be one of the good days. It wasn't.

Turning Point

I failed. I asked to retake the exam—I could prove I had the vision—and was denied. The Navy was winding down from Vietnam, pilot demand had dropped, and the door had simply closed. I spent the next two weeks in a fog, depressed and adrift, because I had never once prepared for any other path.

Then a classmate asked me a question that changed everything: "What are you going to do?"

I turned it back on him. "What is the hardest thing you can do in the Navy?"

"Nuclear power," he said. "Submarines. Nuclear power, but you are not prepared for the difficulties associated with it."

I responded, "I will do that."

I hadn't taken the right engineering courses. I wasn't academically positioned for it. None of that mattered to me in that moment. I made the decision on the spot: I was going nuclear. I spent my final three semesters overloading my coursework, stacking the most demanding engineering classes I could find, trying to close a gap that my classmates had spent years building.

I won't pretend I finished at the top of the program. I got through it the way you get through something when you're underprepared but unwilling to quit through sheer, unglamorous hard work.

Lesson

What felt like the worst outcome of my Naval Academy years became one of the best things that ever happened to me.

The submarine I was assigned to had an extraordinary crew, officers and enlisted men who became, in every real sense, my people. The work was hard and the environment unforgiving, but I found something I hadn't anticipated: I loved it. A career I had never chosen chose me, and it fit better than the one I had designed for myself.

The eye exam didn't cost me a future. It redirected me toward one I couldn't have imagined standing in that examination room, certain my world had just ended.

The sun came up the next morning. It always does.

I have met many people over the years who carry, somewhere in their history, a version of the failed eye exam. The job they didn't get. The program that rejected them. The relationship that ended before they were ready for it to end. The opportunity that closed on a Tuesday with a phone call in careful, corporate language that meant something entirely different from what it said. Most of them, given enough distance, will tell you the same thing I would tell you about that examination room: it felt, in the moment, like the end. It turned out to be a door.

The door doesn't always look like a door when you're standing in front of it. Sometimes it looks like a wall. Sometimes it looks like a failure. Sometimes it looks like two weeks of fog and a classmate asking a question you weren't expecting. The door is the door regardless of what it looks like. What matters is whether, when it opens, you are willing to walk through it even when it leads somewhere you never planned to go.

Meeting Admiral Rickover

Every career has its gatekeepers. The people whose approval you need before you can proceed, whose standards you must meet before the next door opens. Most gatekeepers are forgotten quickly enough. You pass their test, or you don't, and you move on, and the memory of them fades into the texture of a career that has moved past them.

And then there are the ones you never forget. The ones who were so far outside the ordinary that decades later you still find yourself thinking about the afternoon you sat across from them, wondering what exactly happened and what exactly it meant.

Admiral Hyman Rickover was one of those.

Situation

Admiral Hyman Rickover was the father of the nuclear Navy, brilliant, intimidating, and legendary for making grown men walk out of his office wondering what had just happened to them. A personal interview with Rickover was not a formality. It was a gauntlet.

I walked into mine as a Midshipman at the Naval Academy, having no idea what was coming.

My declared major, Analytical Management, was among Rickover's least favorite. The interview began with him reading the wrong file entirely, addressing me as Midshipman Moe. Once he found the right folder, he pivoted immediately to the meaning of my last name and wanted to know who Peter was. I assumed he meant a distant ancestor. He meant Saint Peter. It went downhill from there.

He reviewed my class standings, introduced me to two of his administrative staff in a manner clearly designed to unsettle me, and at one point, when asked to describe the qualities of a leader, I used the word charisma. That single word brought Rickover out of his chair. The room erupted. I stood there, certain I had just ended my naval career before it started.

I didn't even check the acceptance list afterward. My classmates had to tell me: he took me.

Three Encounters, Three Lessons

Turning Point

Encounter One, the Interview: Rickover accepted me despite, or perhaps because of, an interview that felt like a comedic disaster. Looking back, I was the Admiral's entertainment for the afternoon. He smiled during my interview, which was reportedly rare. Whether he saw something in me or simply enjoyed the spectacle, the outcome was the same: I was in.

Encounter Two, the Sea Trials: Years later, as a junior officer of the watch aboard USS Indianapolis during new construction Alpha Sea trials, Rickover stood next to me as my team recovered from an obligatory reactor scram. He seemed pleased. No theatrics. Just a quiet acknowledgment that the work had been done right. In a career defined by his withering standards, that silence spoke volumes.

Encounter Three, the Engineer's Exam: After passing my Engineer's Exam, the most demanding qualification in the nuclear program, I was pulled from the room before results were announced. My heart sank. In the nuclear Navy, being summoned separately meant one thing: you had violated reactor safety protocol, and Rickover himself was going to remove you from the program.

Instead, he congratulated me. He referenced my class standing, recalled our exchange about Saint Peter from years earlier, took full credit for my success, and dismissed me. As I turned to leave, he called me back.

"Do you still have charisma?"

I told him I did.

What I didn't know until the next day was why Rickover had been so unusually gracious. There was a second person in that office, someone I had glimpsed only at the edge of my vision, too focused on my own fate to look directly. That person, I learned later, was former President Richard Nixon. The Admiral was on his best behavior and performing for the President, not me.

I was too terrified of Rickover to take my eyes off him long enough to notice a president.

A Fourth Encounter: The Maintenance That Changed the Fleet

There is one more encounter with Admiral Rickover, and unlike the first three, it did not involve a room, a conversation, or anything that could be called a meeting. It involved a maintenance item, a very good Master Chief Petty Officer, and a captain who was not initially pleased with either of us.

Nuclear submarines operate under some of the most exacting maintenance standards in any branch of any military in the world. This is not bureaucratic caution. It is engineering realism. The systems aboard a nuclear submarine do not forgive improvisation, and the consequences of a failure at sea are not the kind that can be managed after the fact. Rickover had designed those standards personally, and he enforced them with the same intensity he brought to everything else in the nuclear program.

We were close to finishing the construction of our submarine, the newest in the Navy at that time. As we neared delivery, a scheduled maintenance item appeared on the list; one that was technically required but that, it turned out, virtually no submarine before us had actually performed. The difficulty of the procedure was significant, and the potential for error was real. Earlier submarines had bypassed it. The reasoning was practical and, in retrospect, entirely wrong: the risk of a mistake seemed to outweigh the risk of skipping it.

My Master Chief brought it to me. He was one of the sharpest people I have ever worked with, and also one of the most demanding, which in the nuclear Navy is the combination you want in the person responsible for the technical standards of your division. He believed we should do the maintenance. I told him honestly that we could only proceed with the Captain's permission, and that I doubted the Captain would authorize it this close to delivery.

I was right about the Captain's initial reaction. He was not happy. Not because he was opposed to the maintenance in principle, but because we were close to the finish line, the delivery schedule was real, and the possibility of something going wrong at this stage was exactly the kind of risk a commanding officer does not want to carry. He made his position clear in the way that captains make positions clear, which is to say emphatically and without ambiguity.

And then he authorized it.

He ordered that my Master Chief and I personally supervise every step of the procedure and that we would be held responsible for the outcome. That was not an unusual condition. In the nuclear Navy, authority and accountability travel together. You do not get one without the other.

We did the maintenance. We supervised it exactly as ordered, step by step, the way Rickover's program required.

What the inspection revealed changed the fleet.

The inspectors found a design flaw affecting every submarine in the class. Ours was the first boat to have performed this maintenance, which meant ours was the first boat where this problem had been identified. Every other submarine in the class would need modifications. It was not a small finding. It was a significant one, and it existed in every hull that had bypassed the procedure we had just completed.

Because the discovery happened in direct compliance with Admiral Rickover's maintenance program; the program he had designed and that he held everyone in the nuclear Navy to account for; Rickover ordered that all three of us receive a medal. Not a routine commendation. A medal that ranked higher than what most people aboard that submarine would ever receive.

The maintenance that the Captain initially resisted, that previous submarines quietly bypassed, that my Master Chief insisted we perform, turned out to matter in ways none of us fully anticipated when we began it.

Lesson

Four encounters. Four very different versions of the same principle, arriving across the full arc of a career.

What Rickover modeled, from the chaotic first interview to the quiet acknowledgment during sea trials to the congratulations after the Engineer's Exam to the medal that came years later without a conversation at all, was a single consistent belief: standards are not negotiable, and performance is the only currency that matters.

He did not accept me at the interview because I impressed him. He accepted me in spite of how the interview went, perhaps because he saw something beneath the stumbling answers that the grades and the later recovery confirmed. He stood beside me during sea trials and said nothing critical, which in his vocabulary was a form of praise. He took full credit for my success after the Engineer's Exam, recalled a detail from years earlier that I had not expected him to remember, and asked a question that made everyone in the room laugh. And he ordered a medal for a maintenance action he never witnessed, performed by people he likely never thought about again, because they had followed his program exactly and it had mattered.

That last encounter is the one I find most instructive now. Not because of the medal, though the medal meant something. Because of what it revealed about what Rickover had actually built. He was not present for the maintenance. He did not know us by name. He simply had a system, enforced it relentlessly, and trusted that the system would produce results in rooms he could not see, with people he would never meet. When it did, he recognized it. When it did not, he removed it. That consistency, maintained across decades and across an entire Navy, is what made the nuclear program what it was.

The people who hold you to the highest standard are often the ones who believe most in what you are capable of. Rickover was not warm. But he was paying attention. And in his world, that was everything.

Each encounter reveals a principle worth carrying forward. Judgment over presentation: he accepted a midshipman who fumbled every answer because he was evaluating something beneath the surface. Recognition through presence: standing beside a junior officer during a high-stakes recovery and saying nothing critical is its own form of acknowledgment. Accountability with grace: even the most demanding leaders occasionally show you the human being behind the standard, and that moment stays longer than any critique. And finally: systems outlast their architects. The maintenance program Rickover designed kept producing results long after he had turned his attention elsewhere. Build the right system, hold people to it, and trust it to find the things you cannot find yourself.

The Party I Never Expected

There is a particular kind of recognition that no one can arrange for themselves. It cannot be requested, scheduled, or earned through any single act of deliberate effort. It arrives, when it arrives, because of something accumulated over time: something in the way you showed up, day after day, in ways you never expected anyone to notice.

I did not expect anyone to notice.

Situation

When I reported to my first submarine assignment aboard USS Indianapolis (SSN 697), she was still in new construction. I was an Ensign, what the Navy calls a Baby Nuke, and I was, without question, the least experienced person on the boat. Most of my fellow officers were Lieutenants and above, all of them handpicked, all of them several rungs ahead of me in both rank and knowledge. I arrived with my commission, my enthusiasm, and very little else that was immediately useful.

They were glad to see me for exactly that reason. An Ensign is the natural recipient of every task no one else wants, the assignments that need to be done and that fall, by unspoken agreement, to whoever is newest and most eager to prove himself. I embraced this. The unglamorous jobs taught me the submarine from angles that a more comfortable assignment never would have. Systems, procedures, responsibilities I would not have touched for years came to me early, not because I had earned them but because no one else was available.

Very early in that tour, I also learned something that would shape the rest of my career. The enlisted sailors, particularly the Chiefs, the E-7s through E-9s, were not simply experienced. They were exceptional. They had been handpicked by the same rigorous process that selected the officers, and in many cases, they knew more about the systems they maintained than the officers they served under. I made a decision, consciously and deliberately, to treat them accordingly. I listened more than I spoke. I asked more than I directed. I respected what they knew and made clear that I understood the limits of what I did not yet know.

That decision changed the character of my entire tour.

Turning Point

After three and a half years, I received orders to the Navy's Nuclear Power School. It was the right next step professionally, and I accepted it as such. What I had not anticipated was how much it would cost to leave.

A few days before my wife Louise and I departed, two senior enlisted men came to find me. They told me the Chiefs had organized a gathering, an informal one at a private home, to honor us before we left. I asked, out of genuine curiosity, who else would be there.

Just the senior enlisted, they said. No officers.

I stood with that for a moment. This was not a formal ceremony. There was no requirement, no protocol, no chain of command that made this gathering necessary. The Chiefs had organized it entirely on their own initiative, for reasons that were entirely their own. What I came to understand that evening was that they were not honoring me alone. They were honoring Louise.

While I had been learning the submarine, Louise had been building something equally real in the spaces the Navy does not formally recognize. She had sought out the enlisted families, not as a duty, not as a reflection of my rank, but as a genuine expression of who she was. She learned their names. She showed up when things were hard. She treated people with the same warmth and respect whether or not their husband outranked mine, which in most cases he did not. There was no requirement for any of this. The Navy makes no official demand on the spouses of junior officers. She did it because she chose to.

The families felt it. The Chiefs remembered it. And on a quiet evening near the end of our tour, they said so.

Lesson

Leadership, I understood that night, does not stay inside the hull.

It extends into homes and families and the small, unremarkable interactions that happen far from any official record. Louise had led without a title, influenced without authority, and built trust in a community that had every reason to keep its distance from the commanding officer's wife. She had done none of this strategically. She had simply chosen to treat people well, consistently, over time, and the people she treated well had noticed.

The Chiefs' gathering was not on any résumé I have ever written. It did not count toward any promotion, produce any commendation, or appear in any official account of my naval career. What it revealed has stayed with me for the rest of my professional life: the most meaningful recognition is often the recognition you never asked for, extended by people who had no obligation to give it.

Respect is not granted by rank. It is built through how you treat people, especially when no one is watching, and especially when there is no requirement to treat them well at all. And sometimes the most significant leadership in a room is not coming from the person who holds the title.

The early stops do not announce their significance. They deliver it quietly, across years of work and the accumulated weight of people who held you to a standard you were not yet sure you could meet. That is what the first stops are for.

The Nixon reveal belongs here, too, because it speaks to context. I had a former president of the United States in the same room and never once looked at him, because all of my attention was on the man who held my future in his hands. The most important person in any room is not always the most famous one. It is the one whose judgment matters most to what happens next.

Chapter 8

THE FAMILY STOP

Family is the stop that changes the itinerary permanently. Before it, you are traveling more or less alone, building a life organized primarily around your own needs, preferences, and ambitions. After it, you are traveling with other people who did not ask to be on the journey and who depend on you completely, which turns out to be one of the most clarifying experiences a person can have.

What family teaches, more reliably than almost anything else, is what you are actually made of. The patience you thought you had. The generosity you assumed was a settled part of your character. The priorities you believed were fixed. All of these get tested in the family stop, and the results are sometimes surprising in both directions. You discover capacities you did not know you had. You discover limitations you did not want to admit. And in the middle of all of it, if you are paying attention, you discover what actually matters to you, usually because a child has just handed you a picture they drew and looked at you with an expression that contains no ambiguity whatsoever about what they need from you in that moment.

No stop along the way changes a life more completely than the arrival of family. A child reorganizes everything. A marriage is tested and deepened. The people we love most have a way of teaching us what we could not have learned any other way.

The Child That Changes Everything

People will tell you, before you have children, that everything changes when they arrive. They say it with a kind of knowing emphasis that suggests they are transmitting something important. They are. You just cannot receive it yet. The information is accurate. The experience of it is unavailable until it happens, and when it happens, you understand immediately why words kept failing the people who tried to warn you.

Some things have to be lived before they can be understood. The arrival of a first child is one of them.

Situation

Growing up as one of eleven children, I always knew I wanted a family of my own. But first, my wife and I took full advantage of what young married life offers: the freedom to do anything, go anywhere, and answer to no one but each other. Looking back, that season was a gift we didn't fully appreciate until it ended.

Then came the blizzard of 1978.

The Northeast was buried. Connecticut was under a state of emergency. Roads were impassable, the world had gone white and silent, and my wife had chosen this particular moment to go into labor. Getting her to the hospital wasn't just difficult; we nearly didn't make it. I will say this: the possibility of delivering that baby myself on the side of a snow-covered road gave me a level of motivation I had never previously experienced. We were going to reach that hospital.

We made it.

Turning Point

The next morning, our daughter arrived. And they handed her to me.

I don't have adequate words for what I felt in that moment, only that it was immediate, overwhelming, and unlike anything that had come before it. A kind of love that doesn't announce itself gradually. It arrives all at once, and it reorganizes everything.

And right alongside that joy came a thought, clear and quiet: We just changed our lives forever.

Lesson

Freedom is a wonderful thing, and it is also temporary, by design. The life my wife and I enjoyed before our daughter was born wasn't something we lost. It was something we traded up from.

You don't simply add a child to your existing life. You build a new one around them. The responsibility is total, the stakes are permanent, and somehow, in a way that defies easy explanation, it is exactly what you were made for.

She was in our hands now. And we were, without question, better for it.

That reorganization, the one that happens when you hold a child for the first time, is not temporary. It does not fade as the early sleepless weeks give way to a more manageable rhythm. It becomes the operating system on which everything else runs. Every decision that follows, every priority that gets set or reset, every sacrifice that turns out not to feel like a sacrifice, runs on the foundation laid in that moment.

What the blizzard added, in its own chaotic way, was a kind of baptism by urgency. Before she was even born, she had already required something extraordinary from us. She had required us to refuse the obvious obstacles, find the road through the impossible conditions, and arrive at the destination no matter what stood between us and it. That turned out to be good practice.

Parenthood asks for exactly that, over and over, in forms you cannot predict, for the rest of your life. The blizzard was just the first version of the question. Are you willing to do what it takes? We answered it that night on the road to the hospital. We have been answering it ever since.

The Two Televisions

Children have a way of teaching you things at the exact moment you were not expecting a lesson.

Situation

My youngest son was in middle school when he came home one evening, sat down to dinner, and mentioned almost in passing that his class had been assigned to watch the Presidential Debate that night. They would be discussing it the following day. He had a plan for how he intended to watch it.

He wanted to use two televisions.

He explained it simply. One television would be tuned to a channel that leaned Republican in its coverage. The other would be tuned to a channel that leaned Democratic. He wanted to watch the same debate through two different lenses, hear the same exchanges interpreted from opposing perspectives, and then decide for himself what he actually thought.

I asked him why.

He said he wanted to hear both sides before he made up his mind. He wanted to be able to argue the issues from more than one direction. He did not want to arrive at his conclusions because someone else had already arranged the facts for him.

I sat with that for a moment.

He was in middle school. He had arrived at something that a great many adults never quite get to: the understanding that the framing of information shapes the meaning of it, that the same event can be made to look entirely different depending on who is describing it and what they need the description to accomplish, and that the only reliable defense against that is to seek out the other side before you decide.

I told him it was a good plan. What I did not tell him, because he did not need the editorial commentary from his father at that particular moment, was that I was genuinely proud of what I had just heard.

Not proud in the reflexive way of a parent whose child has said something pleasing. Proud in the specific way you feel when someone you love demonstrates a quality you were not sure the world was still producing: intellectual honesty. The willingness to be inconvenienced by a perspective that does not confirm what you already think. The discipline to seek out the argument you disagree with before you dismiss it.

Turning Point

He watched both televisions that night. He came to his own conclusions. He went to school the following day, prepared to engage from multiple angles.

I went to bed thinking about the lesson my son had just taught me without meaning to.

I have always believed that I approach questions with reasonable balance. That belief is easier to maintain when you are not being shown, by a middle school student at the dinner table, what genuine balance actually looks like in practice. He had not simply heard both sides. He had deliberately sought them out, designed his own system for receiving them simultaneously, and trusted himself to evaluate what he found.

I was not sure I had always done the same.

That evening stayed with me for years. When I sat down to write *The Facts Don't Matter*, the book that argues that how we interpret information is at least as consequential as the information itself, I kept returning to that image: my son in the living room, two televisions on, deciding for himself. It was not the argument of the book. It was the spirit of it. The insistence that the facts you receive are always packaged in a frame, that the frame is always someone else's choice, and that wisdom begins when you start asking what the same facts look like in a different frame before you accept the first one you were handed.

He did not know he was doing any of this. He just knew he wanted to hear both sides. That is, in my experience, where most genuine wisdom begins.

Lesson

The stop that family provides is not always the dramatic one. It is not always the blizzard and the hospital and the reorganization of everything. Sometimes it is an ordinary Tuesday evening, a dinner table, and a child who has figured out something you have been working on longer than he has been alive.

My son was not trying to teach me anything that night. He was trying to do his homework. What he gave me was a model I have carried since: seek the other perspective before you conclude, not as an obligation to fairness but as a genuine act of self-interest. The person who understands the opposing argument is harder to mislead, harder to manipulate, and more capable of arriving at something that resembles the truth than the person who has only ever heard one version of it.

He is, as I write this, a grown man building his own life. I have never told him that the evening he watched two televisions became a chapter in how I think. Perhaps he will read it here.

If so, thank you. You were ahead of me on that one.

Chapter 9

THE UNEXPECTED STOPS

We plan for arrivals. We plan for departures. We plan for the milestones we can see coming from a reasonable distance. What we almost never plan for is the unexpected stop, the moment when life pulls the car to the side of the road for reasons that have nothing to do with our schedule and everything to do with something we did not see coming.

The unexpected stop is the most instructive kind, precisely because it is the one we have not prepared remarks for. When the planned thing happens, we respond with the response we rehearsed. When the unplanned thing happens, we respond with whatever we actually are. This is useful information, even when, especially when, what it reveals is less flattering than we would have preferred.

The stories in this chapter are about unexpected stops of various kinds: a job that disappeared, a tornado on the first week of a new assignment, a traffic jam that became a daily education in what we can and cannot control. Each one required a response that the situation itself had not provided a script for. Each one taught something that the planned stops could not have.

Not every stop is planned. Some of the most instructive ones arrive as setbacks, redirections, and events that bear no resemblance to anything we put on the map. These are the stops that test us most and teach us most, often at the same time.

The Lost Job That Became a Gift

There is a version of professional life where everything proceeds according to plan: the promotions arrive on schedule, the opportunities materialize as expected, and the path from where you are to where you intend to be stays reasonably clear. Most people who have spent significant time in organizations will tell you that this version exists mostly in the imagination. The actual version involves detours, retractions, reversals, and occasional periods of sitting quietly in a reduced position, wondering what happened to the plan.

The leaders I have respected most over a long career are not the ones whose paths were smooth. They are the ones who handled the rough stretches without losing their integrity, their composure, or their willingness to keep contributing regardless of what the organization had recently done to their expectations.

Situation

Early in my business career, I was promoted from a sales to a leadership position. This was not a gentle transition. I took over an operation that was stable but not meeting expectations. I learned how to lead inside that job, and I loved it. I could see myself expanding my territory, building something that would allow my young family to put down roots.

Imagine my surprise when the President of our company flew in for dinner with my wife and me. I was naive enough not to ask why a sitting president would make a special trip. I found out quickly: they were impressed with my work and wanted me to come to the Home Office to take over a crucial position.

The role came with a significant pay cut. The agreement was for three years: serve the Home Office tour, then return to a larger operation. The math worked if everything held. I took the job.

Turning Point

Halfway through the tour, the CEO called me in and offered to accelerate my path, jumping me one or two levels of the corporate hierarchy in a single move. I agreed on the spot. The Home Office tour was demanding and meaningful work, and I gave it everything I had.

Then something changed. The leadership team decided I should complete my Home Office tour, and the field job that had been offered was retracted.

I had a choice in that moment about how to respond. I could have pushed back, registered my frustration, and made clear that the retraction was not a small thing. I accepted it instead. I finished the tour. I trusted that the organization was watching how I handled the disappointment as carefully as it had watched how I handled the success.

Lesson

The career I had mapped from that field office would have been a good career. What I could not see from inside it was how much larger the path became once I was willing to leave it.

How we handle the retraction of an opportunity often matters more than how we pursued it. Organizations have long memories for grace under pressure. The executive who accepts a setback without making it someone else's problem is almost always the one the organization finds a way to reward when the timing is right.

Patience is not passive. In the right circumstances, it is the most strategic decision a leader can make.

There is something else worth naming here, something that took me longer to appreciate than the professional lesson. The pay cut I accepted to take the Home Office role was real. The sacrifice was real. The retraction of the offer I had been given was real, and it stung in the way that broken promises sting even when they are broken without malice. None of that was nothing.

But the posture I maintained through all of it, the decision to absorb the disappointment without making it into a grievance, to continue performing at the same level after the incentive had been modified, to trust the organization even when the organization had given me reason to be skeptical, turned out to be the most important professional investment I ever made. Not because the organization rewarded it perfectly. But because it kept me intact as a person. The alternative, bitterness, withdrawal, the slow corrosion of someone who has decided they are owed something they are not receiving, costs far more than it ever recovers. I have watched that happen to talented people. It is one of the saddest things a career can do to a person.

The Weather Problem

Leadership is tested most clearly not in the moments we prepare for but in the ones we don't. The crisis drill, the rehearsed presentation, the carefully managed performance review: these reveal competence. What reveals character is the tornado on the first week of a new assignment, in a city you don't yet know, with your new bosses in the back seat.

Situation

I had been selected for a top executive position reporting directly to our President, and I had barely arrived before the first test appeared. A high-level dinner had been arranged in downtown Fort Worth. A storm system was threatening the area, which prompted the group to relocate to Arlington, between Fort Worth and Dallas. The other executives suggested I drive, probably to help me learn the Metroplex.

The dinner was productive and collegial. Storm sirens sounded at one point, but Arlington remained safe. Then, as we prepared to leave, word came: a tornado had touched down in Fort Worth. Multiple accidents on the roads. Trucks overturned. Hazardous conditions in every direction.

I was behind the wheel. My passengers were my new bosses. And I was driving in a city I did not yet fully know, in the dark, after a tornado, with every traffic light out.

Turning Point

As I approached the interstate I could see it, the red wash of brake lights stretching further than made any sense. Something told me not to merge. Not a calculation. A sixth sense, the kind that experienced leaders learn to trust even when they cannot explain it.

I pulled off to the side of the road. In the sweep of the headlights I saw an opening, not a road, just a gap in a field that suggested a path through to something on the other side. I had no idea where it led. I took the opening. We navigated through the darkness by instinct and incremental decision-making, each turn revealing just enough of the next stretch to keep moving. We arrived in a relatively short time.

What we learned afterward: the interstate we had avoided was at a standstill for more than five hours. And the restaurant where the dinner had originally been planned, before the group relocated to Arlington, had taken a direct hit from the tornado.

Lesson

The interstate was the obvious route. It was also, that night, a five-hour parking lot. The instinct to pull off and find another way was not dramatic or heroic. It was the willingness to trust accumulated judgment over the comfort of the familiar path, even when the alternative was a field with no road in it.

There is also a quieter lesson in the restaurant that wasn't. The original plan would have placed us somewhere the tornado found. Not every detour is a problem. Some of them are precisely where we were supposed to go.

The field with no road in it has become, over the years, one of my most reliable mental images for the kind of judgment that matters most under pressure. Not the judgment that consults every available option and weighs each one carefully before selecting the optimal path. The judgment that reads a situation in real time, trusts what it sees, and acts on that trust even when the action requires leaving the known route for a dark field in the middle of a Texas night.

That kind of judgment cannot be taught in a classroom. It develops through accumulated experience of making decisions in conditions that don't cooperate, noticing what works and what doesn't, and building over time the kind of internal compass that doesn't require a map because it has absorbed so many of them.

The Traffic Jam Lesson

We tend to measure our responses to frustration by whether they solve the problem. If I am stuck in traffic and I find an alternate route that gets me there faster, the alternate route was a good idea. If it turns out to be slower, it was a bad one. This is a reasonable framework as far as it goes, but it misses something important:

the quality of our experience is not always determined by the outcome. Sometimes it is determined by the simple fact of moving versus sitting still, of choosing a response versus absorbing a condition.

The I-4 story is not really a story about traffic. It is a story about what we do with the things we cannot change.

Situation

For several years, my professional life was divided between two offices, one in downtown Tampa, one in Orlando, and the road between them was Interstate 4. Those of you who know I-4 are already nodding. There is exactly one direct route connecting those two cities, and on any given day it can be one of the most reliably frustrating stretches of highway in Florida.

I am not, by nature, a patient man in a traffic backup. Sitting still while the clock moves and the car doesn't produce a particular variety of frustration that is disproportionate to the actual stakes involved and entirely immune to reason.

So, I did what an impatient person with a good memory and enough repetitions does: I started mapping the alternatives. Through accumulated observation, I built a mental library of two-lane county roads and surface streets that could route around the worst of it.

Turning Point

At some point, I realized something worth examining. I was almost certainly not saving time. The two-lane roads with their stop signs and school zones were not, in any objective sense, faster than the interstate I had abandoned.

But I was arriving differently.

Lesson

I-4 was not going to change. The traffic was not going to thin because I needed it to. What was negotiable was my response to it. The back-roads didn't save time. They saved something more valuable: the mental and emotional state I needed to do my job well once I arrived. A leader who walks into the office already depleted by circumstances he couldn't control has less to give the people waiting for him.

The orange groves were something, as it turned out. Some mornings, they were the best part of the commute.

There is a broader application here that extends well past the Florida highway system. Every professional life contains its version of I-4: the situation that isn't going to improve, the colleague who isn't going to change, the organizational reality that isn't going to bend to your preference, no matter how reasonable your preference is. The people who thrive in those situations are rarely the ones who found a way to fix the unfixable. They are the ones who found a way to respond to it that left them intact enough to do good work when they arrived.

That is not resignation. It is strategy. The orange groves were the strategy. The two-lane roads with their stop signs and their school zones and their unhurried pace were the strategy. Getting there five minutes later but arriving as yourself rather than as a depleted version of yourself was the strategy. I didn't know that at the time. I thought I was just avoiding traffic. It took a few years to understand what I was actually doing.

The Late-Life Reinvention

Situation

One of the quiet privileges of graduating from the Naval Academy is that you spend the rest of your life connected to a group of people who went through something hard together and never quite lost the thread. The tailgate gatherings before Navy football games had a way of pulling us back together across decades and distance.

By the time many of us were moving through our late fifties and early sixties, the careers that had taken decades to build were reaching their conclusions. CEOs stepping back. Admirals and Generals completing their final tours. Physicians, executives, senior government officials, people who had spent their entire adult lives in rooms where serious decisions were made, were standing at the threshold of a life without a title, without a mission, without a Monday morning that required anything of them.

I started asking a question at those tailgates: *What do you plan to do in retirement?*

The answers fell into four categories with remarkable consistency: travel, grandchildren and family, hobbies, like golf and tennis, cruises, and catching up on everything around the house that demanding careers had left undone. The list was reasonable, well-earned, and almost universally the same.

I listened carefully. Then I asked the follow-up question: *What are you going to do after that?*

The table went quiet every time.

Turning Point

No one had an answer. What they had, uniformly, was a question back at me: *Why do you ask?*

I explained where the question came from. In financial planning, one of the foundational calculations is longevity, how long a person is likely to live, and whether their resources can keep pace with that timeline. Someone retiring at sixty with reasonable health was not planning for a decade of leisure. They were planning for twenty-five or thirty years of life that needed to mean something.

Those four answers are wonderful things. But they are not a twenty-five-year plan. They are, at most, a few years of well-deserved decompression before the deeper question arrives and insists on being answered: Now what?

The classmates who had spent careers leading organizations and developing people had more to offer than a bucket list. They simply hadn't thought past the first chapter of what came next.

When they turned the question back on me, I told them the truth: I wasn't certain of the specifics yet, but I was certain of one thing. I would not leave the workforce entirely. Not because I had to. Because the work I found, working alongside people I genuinely liked, doing something I believed in, never felt like something I needed to escape.

Someone said it better than I ever could: *when you find the right job for you, you won't have to work another day in your life.*

Lesson

The most accomplished people in any room are not automatically the most prepared for what comes after accomplishment. Success, for most of a career, answers the question of purpose by default. The mission is the meaning. When the mission ends, the question resurfaces, and the people who were best at the job are sometimes the least prepared for the transition away from it.

Reinvention later in life is not about finding something to fill the time. It is about finding something worthy of the person you have spent a lifetime becoming. The skills, the judgment, the hard-won perspective that took decades to develop do not expire at retirement. They are, in many ways, at their most valuable precisely when the formal career ends, if the person holding them is willing to find a new arena for them.

The tailgate conversations were never really about football.

What those conversations revealed, over and over, was a gap that most high-achieving people never see coming: the gap between being finished with a career and being finished with a purpose. These were extraordinary people by any measure. They had led organizations, shaped industries, served their country, and built things that outlasted them. And they were standing at the edge of thirty years of unstructured time with a list of four activities that would fill, at most, three years of it.

The follow-up question, what are you going to do after that, is not meant to be unkind. It is meant to be useful. It is the question that financial planners ask about portfolios: not just whether you have enough, but whether what you have is built to last as long as you will. The same question applies to purpose. Is what you are planning to do with your post-career life built to sustain you for the full duration? For most people who have not thought carefully about it, the honest answer is no. The good news is that it is almost never too late to think carefully about it.

Part III

THE DRIVERS OF HAPPINESS

The qualities that make the difference between a life endured and a life enjoyed.

A Note on Part III

After a career spent teaching and coaching leaders and studying what separates people who thrive from people who merely survive, I have come to believe that seven qualities matter more than any others when it comes to lasting happiness: perspective, relationships, purpose, gratitude, resilience, humor, and service. The chapters that follow explore each one through story, because stories carry truth in ways that lists and frameworks cannot. The first five are followed by Humor and Lightheartedness and Service, and Helping Others Helps Us which allow us to further understand what it takes to be ultimately happy.

Chapter 10

PERSPECTIVE

Perspective is the least expensive upgrade available to a human being. It requires no new resources, no additional time, no change in circumstances. It requires only the willingness to look at what is already there from a different angle, to ask what this situation would look like to someone standing elsewhere, to consider whether the story you are telling yourself about what is happening is the only story available.

This is, of course, easier to describe than to practice. In the middle of a genuine difficulty, the invitation to shift perspective can feel dismissive, like being told to look on the bright side when the bright side is not currently visible from where you are standing. This chapter is not making that argument. It is making a more specific one: that the lens through which we view our circumstances is not fixed, that we have more authorship over our experience than we typically exercise, and that the people who consistently demonstrate this capacity tend to navigate their lives with a quality of equanimity that is worth understanding and worth developing.

Two stories. One about a flight that didn't make it across the Atlantic. One about a professional setback that looked, for several years, like a failure, before revealing itself as a redirect. Both are about the same thing: what becomes visible when you look at the same event through a different lens.

Of all the drivers of happiness, perspective may be the most immediately available. We cannot always change our circumstances. We cannot always improve our finances, repair our relationships, or undo our mistakes. But we can almost always change the lens through which we view what is happening to us.

This is not the same as positive thinking. Perspective does not require pretending things are better than they are. It requires recognizing that two people in identical circumstances can experience them entirely differently depending on what they know, what they assume, and where they choose to direct their attention.

The Airline Delay Story

The same event, experienced by two people with different information, produces two entirely different emotional realities. One person's minor annoyance is another person's profound relief. One person's four-hour delay is another person's narrow escape from something considerably worse. The event does not change. The experience of it changes completely depending on what you know and where you direct your attention.

I learned this lesson in the clearest possible way on a transatlantic flight that did not make it to the Atlantic.

Situation

I have logged more miles in the air than I can count, regular flights between Texas and Florida, and years of international travel as part of my work. If you fly enough, delays stop being surprises and start being taxes. You pay them and move on.

But one evening out of Charlotte, North Carolina, I got a delay story worth keeping.

My wife and I were flying to Frankfurt with friends on an overnight transatlantic flight. We pushed back on schedule, climbed smoothly into the night sky, and I was settling in when something outside my window caught my eye. A flash. Then what looked unmistakably like an engine on fire.

I said nothing. Then I noticed the flight attendant near me touch her earpiece, and something in her expression changed. She reached for her seatbelt and shoulder harness, stood up quickly, and promptly caught her arm in the harness on the way up. She went straight down to the floor, flailing in a tangle of straps and urgency.

Under the circumstances, a possible engine fire, an unannounced emergency, an ocean crossing ahead of us, I should not have found this funny. I found it very funny.

Turning Point

From the cockpit, not a word about fire. Not a word about an emergency. The pilot's only announcement was calm, measured, and almost casual: we would be returning to Charlotte. That was all.

Most passengers heard a minor inconvenience. I had seen the flash. I knew what returning to Charlotte actually meant. And yet the pilots, who knew everything I knew and considerably more, offered nothing but composure. We landed without incident. The airline got us back in the air four hours later.

Lesson

Two groups of people experienced the exact same event that night. The passengers were mildly annoyed about the delay. I was quietly aware that we had returned with an engine on fire. And the pilots, carrying the full weight of what was actually happening, were the calmest people on the aircraft.

That is perspective in its purest form.

Most of the people on that plane traveled to Frankfurt and complained about a 4-hour delay in Charlotte. I traveled gratefully that we went back at all. Perspective is not determined by circumstances. It is determined by the person holding them.

The pilots are worth returning to for a moment because what they modeled that night goes beyond perspective into something closer to professional grace. They were carrying information that would have terrified the cabin if they shared it fully. They chose instead to share what was necessary, nothing more, nothing less, and to do it in a tone that communicated exactly what the situation required: calm competence in the presence of genuine difficulty. That is not deception. That is leadership. The information served no one by being delivered in a way that caused panic. The calm served everyone.

I think about those pilots often when I am in a leadership situation where I hold information that others don't, and where my tone and framing will shape the experience of everyone in the room. The cabin follows the cockpit. If the cockpit is calm, the cabin can be calm. If the cockpit loses composure, the cabin loses it faster and harder. Perspective is personal. But the perspective we project is also a gift, or a burden, that we give to everyone around us. Choose accordingly.

The Setback That Was a Redirect

Some events look like one thing for several years and then reveal themselves to be something else entirely. The failure that was actually a course correction. The rejection that was actually protection from a path that would not have served you. The door that closed in a way that felt, at the time, definitive, and that turned out to be a door to a hallway that led to a room you could not have found any other way.

Perspective, in these cases, is not something you can manufacture in the moment. It requires time. The lesson of this story is that time, applied to a setback, often reveals that the setback was doing something you didn't understand while it was happening.

Situation

Elena had spent eleven years building what she considered the defining work of her professional life: a curriculum development practice that served mid-sized nonprofits across the country. She started it with a laptop and a spare bedroom and grew it to a team of seven, with clients in fourteen states and a waiting list she was proud of. The work was meaningful. The clients were genuine partners. She went to sleep most nights satisfied in the specific way that people are satisfied when the work they do matches the reason they got into it.

The financial collapse came the way these things come: quickly, then all at once. Two anchor clients lost their funding in the same quarter, a domino effect that began with a federal grant program that was restructured and ended with Elena sitting in her car in a parking garage on a Wednesday afternoon, staring at a spreadsheet that stopped making sense no matter which direction she read it.

She held on for eight months. She renegotiated contracts, cut her own salary to nothing, and converted two team members to part-time. In the end, the practice could not be saved on the timeline that the bills required. She dissolved it on a March morning and spent the following three months doing what people do in those circumstances: applying for positions she was overqualified for, taking consulting work she found uninspiring, and carrying the particular weight of a person who had built something real and watched it become past tense.

She described that period, years later, as the longest she ever felt genuinely lost. Not sad exactly. Lost. The compass she had been navigating by was gone, and she did not yet have a new one.

Turning Point

The call came from a university in her city. They were building a new center for nonprofit leadership and were looking for someone to design its flagship training program. A former client had given her name. The position was not exactly what she had done before. It was larger, more structured, better resourced, and attached to an institution with the kind of staying power that a seven-person practice could never have.

She almost did not apply. She spent eleven years building something independent, and the idea of working within an institution felt like a retreat from the version of herself she worked hard to become. She applied because a friend told her she was an idiot, which was the kind of direct assessment that only certain friendships can deliver and that Elena, to her credit, was still capable of receiving.

She got the position. Within two years, the program she designed was serving more nonprofits annually than her practice served in its best year. Within four years, it trained over a thousand practitioners across seventeen states. The waiting list she had once been proud of looked, from this vantage point, like a very small version of what the work had been trying to become.

Lesson

Elena is careful when she tells this story, not to make the collapse sound like it was secretly fine. It was not fine. It cost her savings, her team, and three months of genuine disorientation that she does not romanticize in retrospect. The loss was real.

What she came to understand, with the perspective that only time provides, is that the practice she built was a prototype. It was doing the right work at a scale that could not ultimately sustain itself, and the collapse, as painful as it was, created the conditions for that work to find an institution strong enough to carry it further than she could have carried it alone.

She did not know this while she was sitting in the parking garage. She could not have known it. Perspective of this kind is not available at the moment of the setback. It requires the willingness to survive the setback without concluding, prematurely, that the story is over. The story was not over. It was between chapters. The next chapter turned out to be better than anything she had outlined.

The gift of hindsight is not available on demand. But what is available on demand is the decision not to let the current chapter be the final verdict. The parking garage moment is real. The spreadsheet that stopped making sense is real. None of it is the whole story. The perspective that allows you to hold that possibility, even when it is not visible, is one of the most useful things a human being can cultivate.

Chapter 11

RELATIONSHIPS

The science of happiness has produced a great many contested findings over the past several decades. Experts disagree about the role of income, about the contribution of genetics, about whether experiences make us happier than possessions, and by how much. These debates are genuine, and the evidence is often genuinely ambiguous.

On one finding, however, the evidence is not ambiguous at all. The quality of our relationships is the single strongest predictor of how happy and how healthy we are over the course of a lifetime. Not our income. Not our achievements. Not our health habits, though those matter too. The people we are connected to, and the depth and authenticity of those connections, determine more about how a life feels from the inside than almost any other factor researchers have been able to identify.

This finding is well known. It is also, in practice, routinely underinvested in. We spend enormous energy on the things that matter less, the career, the accumulation, the optimization of the visible parts of our lives, and comparatively little on the relationships that research consistently identifies as the foundation of everything. The stories in this chapter are about what happens when someone gets that priority right, and what becomes available to us when we close the distance rather than maintain it.

The Harvard Study of Adult Development, one of the longest-running studies of human life ever conducted, followed men for more than eighty years and arrived at a simple conclusion: good relationships keep us happier and healthier. Not wealth. Not fame. Not achievement. Relationships.

The friend who shows up. The family member who calls every week. The colleague who asks a real question and stays for the real answer. These are the people who make a life.

The Friend Who Showed Up

Adult friendship is a strange and underappreciated thing. We tend to invest our thinking about relationships in the romantic ones, the family ones, and the professional ones that have obvious stakes attached to them. Adult friendship exists in a different category: voluntary, unstructured, sustained by nothing more binding than mutual affection and the periodic decision to make time for each other.

That lightness is friendship's greatest strength. It is also its greatest vulnerability. When life gets demanding, which it does, adult friendships are often the first relationships to get quietly deprioritized. There is no contract, no obligation, no consequence for drifting. The drift can go on for years before either person notices how far it has gone. And then one of you ends up drowning quietly, in plain sight, surrounded by people who care and don't know how to say so.

Marcus knew how to say so. He just didn't say it with words.

Situation

Daniel had known Marcus for nearly twenty years. They met early in their careers, bonded over bad coffee in a conference room somewhere, and stayed connected through the usual rhythms of adult friendship, the occasional lunch, the text on a birthday, the promise to get together soon that sometimes kept and sometimes didn't.

Then Daniel's world came apart.

His marriage ended after twenty-three years. The house went on the market. His oldest daughter stopped returning his calls for a while. He kept going to work because work was the one place where he still knew who he was. He smiled in meetings. He hit his numbers. He told anyone who asked that he was doing fine.

He was not doing fine.

What made it harder was the silence. Not hostile silence, just the particular quiet that surrounds a man in crisis when the people around him don't know what to say and so say nothing. Everyone was being considerate. Daniel had never felt more alone in a room full of people who cared about him.

Turning Point

On a Thursday afternoon, for no particular reason, no anniversary, no trigger Daniel could identify, Marcus called. Not a text. A call.

He said: "I'm coming through your city Saturday. I've got about four hours. Let's have lunch, and then I want to see where you're living now."

It wasn't a question.

He showed up on Saturday. They had lunch. They drove past the house Daniel no longer lived in, which was harder than Daniel expected and somehow easier because someone was sitting in the passenger seat. Marcus didn't try to fix anything. He just stayed for four hours and then drove home.

Daniel sat in his apartment that evening and realized it was the first time in months he felt like himself.

Lesson

Marcus didn't say anything particularly wise that Saturday. The act of showing up was the wisdom.

We remember the people who showed up. Not the ones who meant to, not the ones who thought about it, not the ones who sent the right words at the right time. The ones who got in the car.

Relationships are not maintained by intention. They are built by presence and sometimes rebuilt by a single Saturday afternoon that nobody planned, and nobody forgot.

There is a question worth sitting with after reading this story: who in your life right now is the equivalent of Daniel in that apartment? Who is doing fine in the way that means they are not doing fine, surrounded by people who are being considerate and waiting for a cue and sending texts and meaning to reach out? You probably know someone. Most of us do. The question is not whether we care about them. The question is whether we are going to close the distance or keep the comfortable one.

Marcus did not do anything heroic. He made a phone call and drove to a city he was passing through anyway and stayed for four hours. The heroism is in the decision to prioritize it, to treat that Saturday afternoon as something that mattered enough to show up for when plenty of reasonable alternatives existed. The gift was not the visit. The gift was the decision that the visit was worth making.

The Phone Call That Took Almost Twenty Years

Paul and Eddie had not spoken in nineteen years when Paul picked up the phone.

They had been close in the way that young men are close when they are thrown together by circumstance and discover, against their own expectations, that they genuinely like each other. College roommates freshman year, then by choice every year after that. They attended each other's weddings. They had been present at the births of first children, stood in hospital waiting rooms making bad jokes to manage the tension, called each other from payphones and then cell phones across the various distances that careers and moves had put between them.

And then, the way it sometimes happens without any single decisive event to point to, they had drifted. Paul moved twice. Eddie changed jobs three times. The calls became less frequent, then occasional, then the kind of thing that happened at Christmas if someone remembered. Then not even that.

Nineteen years.

Paul could not have told you precisely when the friendship ended because it had not ended. It simply stopped. There was a difference, he thought, though he would have struggled to explain it. An ending has a moment. A stopping just has a last time, which neither person recognizes as the last time until years later, when they are trying to remember when they last spoke and cannot quite land on it.

He thought about Eddie with some regularity. Not constantly, not with any particular weight of grief, but the way you think about a room you used to spend time in. A mild, occasional awareness that something good had been in your life and was no longer, through no cause you could specifically name.

The thing that made him pick up the phone on a Wednesday in February was nothing dramatic. He had seen a photograph on the internet of a place they had driven through together twenty-five years ago, a diner in a small town in Pennsylvania that neither of them had any particular reason to visit except that they had been driving and hungry and it had been there. He remembered the specific quality of the afternoon. The light. The terrible coffee that Eddie drank two cups of anyway. Something Eddie had said made Paul laugh until his eyes watered.

He found the number. He was not entirely sure it would still work.

It worked.

Eddie answered on the third ring with the particular wariness of someone receiving a call from an unknown number. Then Paul said his name, and there was a pause of approximately two seconds, and then Eddie said, "I was wondering when one of us was going to do that."

They talked for two hours and forty minutes. Paul timed it accidentally because he had to leave for a meeting and kept not leaving. They covered twenty years in the way that old friends cover time, which is to say they skipped most of it and went directly to the parts that mattered. Children. Parents who aged. Work that had been meaningful and work that had been a mistake. One health scare each, delivered with the careful lightness of men who had processed the fear and were now offering the story rather than the emotion.

At some point near the end, Eddie said, "I don't know why we stopped."

"I don't either," Paul said.

"We shouldn't have."

"No," Paul said. "We shouldn't have."

This was the entire post-mortem. Neither of them needed more than that.

They have spoken every three weeks since. Not every week, which would be ambitious for two men in their mid-fifties with full lives and genuine demands on their time. Every three weeks, which turns out to be enough to maintain the thing rather than rebuild it each time from scratch.

Paul thought about what the nineteen years cost him. Not in dramatic terms, not with the weight of genuine regret, but with the honest acknowledgment of a man who now understands something he did not understand when the drift began: adult friendships do not maintain themselves. They require, at a minimum, the occasional decision to pick up the phone. The drift is always available. It requires no effort, no choice, no intention. It simply happens in the spaces where intention is absent.

The reconnection required one phone call. Paul had been capable of making that call for nineteen years. He thought about it, in the vague way he thought about Eddie when a photograph of a Pennsylvania diner surfaced on the internet, and had not made it, and then another year had passed.

The call took nine minutes to justify and two hours and forty minutes to complete.

He does not know what he was waiting for. He suspects he was waiting for nothing in particular, which is to say he was waiting for a reason not to have to be the one who reached out first, which is a waiting game that two people can play simultaneously and indefinitely until one of them decides to stop playing it.

He stopped playing it on a Wednesday in February because of a photograph of a diner.

He is glad he did.

The lesson he carries is not that he should have called sooner, though he should have. It is that the call was always available.

The nineteen years were a gap, not a verdict. Old friendships have a particular quality of durability that newer ones have not yet earned: they do not require explanation or warm-up. You call, the other person answers, and you are both immediately back in the room you used to share, because the room was never really locked. It was only closed.

You have to be the one to open it.

The Chance Encounter

We tend to think of the people who shape us as the ones we chose deliberately: the mentors we sought out, the coaches we hired, the teachers whose courses we enrolled in. And those people matter enormously. But alongside them, if we are honest about our own histories, there are the ones we didn't choose at all. The person who sat next to us on a delayed flight and said something that we have been thinking about ever since. The stranger in a waiting room who asked a question that opened something we had been keeping closed. The chance encounter that turned out to be anything but.

These encounters happen because life is not as organized as our calendars suggest. The most significant conversations are not always the scheduled ones.

Situation

Nathan had been in the airport for two hours longer than he intended to be. The delay was mechanical, the kind of explanation that is technically informative and practically useless. Gate B-22 at San Diego International had filled with the particular energy of people recalibrating their afternoons.

Nathan was forty-four years old, and in the middle of a career transition he had not entirely chosen. The consulting firm he had built over eleven years had been acquired eight months earlier. He had meetings scheduled in Atlanta. Conversations that might become opportunities. Nothing confirmed, nothing certain, the whole trip carrying the anxiety of a man who had spent two decades knowing exactly what he did and was now auditioning answers to a question he used to find easy: What do you do?

The laptop was open, but nothing was getting written.

"Is anyone sitting here?"

An older man, mid-seventies, with the unhurried bearing of someone who had long since stopped being rattled by delayed flights, gestured at the empty seat beside him. Nathan moved his bag.

Turning Point

His name was Gerald. He spent the first half of his career in corporate law, successful, well-compensated, and quietly suffocating. At forty-six, he had left, not with a crisis or a manifesto, but with the patient certainty of someone who finally admitted something he had known for years.

What he had been drawn back to, consistently, was the architecture of how people learn. He spent the second half of his career building leadership development programs, work that he woke up thinking about in the way he never once woke up thinking about a legal brief.

"The mistake I almost made," Gerald said, "was waiting for someone to hand me the answer. Clarity doesn't come from the outside in. It comes from the inside out. You're not asking yourself the right question yet."

"What's the right question?"

Gerald thought about it. "Not what should I do next. That one sends you in circles. The better question is, what have I kept coming back to, even when I was doing something else? The answer to that one is usually pretty short. And usually already true."

On the flight home, somewhere over the Gulf Coast, Nathan wrote three words on the back of a boarding pass: *What keeps returning.*

Lesson

He launched an executive coaching practice fourteen months later. It was smaller than the consulting firm, less impressive on paper, and more meaningful than anything he had built before it.

The chance encounter has always been one of life's most underrated teachers, precisely because it arrives without credentials, without agenda, and without any obligation on either side to make it matter. Close the laptop. Move the bag. Let the stranger sit down. Some of the most important mentoring any of us will ever do is for people whose names we will never remember.

Gerald's question, what have I kept coming back to even when I was doing something else, is worth returning to regardless of whether you are in the middle of a career transition. It is a question worth asking on an ordinary Tuesday, not because anything is wrong, but because the answer has a way of drifting over time, and it is useful to recalibrate. The thing you kept coming back to at thirty-five may be different from the thing you keep coming back to at fifty. Both are worth knowing.

There is also something in this story about the quality of attention we bring to the people we find ourselves next to. Gerald could have opened his book and stayed in it. Most people would have. What made him different was the willingness to notice that the man beside him was carrying something, and to offer, without agenda and without expectation of anything in return, the thing that might help. That is not a complicated skill. It is a rare one. And it is available to any of us on any given afternoon when we choose to close the laptop, move the bag, and let the stranger sit down.

Almost Fifty Years, Thirty of Which Were Happy

I come from a family that knows something about long marriages.

On my father's side, his parents were married for more than sixty years. My own parents' marriage lasted until death separated them, which is the only way it ended. I grew up watching couples stay, work through things, and arrive somewhere on the other side of difficulty that looked, from the outside, like something worth having.

When people ask how long my wife and I have been married, I tell them we are approaching fifty years, of which about thirty were happy. They always laugh. And then they wait, because they can feel there is something underneath the joke.

Here is what is underneath it.

Long marriages are not uniformly happy. Anyone who tells you otherwise has either a very short memory or a very selective one. Fifty years of marriage contain seasons of genuine joy and seasons of genuine difficulty, and the difficulty is not a sign that the marriage is failing. It is a sign that the marriage is real. Two people, living close, building a life together, raising children, navigating careers and losses, and the accumulated weight of decades, this is not a situation that produces only harmony. It produces the full range of human experience, including conflict, including disappointment, including the occasional period where you look across the table and wonder, with perfect sincerity, how you ended up here.

The thirty-year line is not a confession of regret. It is an acknowledgment that the other twenty years existed, that they were hard in various ways, and that working through them was what made the thirty years possible.

I believe it is more difficult to have long marriages today than it was for my parents' and grandparents' generation, and I think the reasons are worth naming honestly.

Part of it is the absence of role models. When you grow up watching grandparents who have been married for sixty years, and parents whose marriage lasted until one of them died, you absorb something about what commitment looks like over time. You understand, from lived example, that the difficult season is a season. That it passes. Without those examples, the difficult season can look like a verdict rather than a chapter.

Part of it is the ease of dissolution. I am not suggesting that all marriages should last forever regardless of circumstances. Some marriages end for good and necessary reasons, and the ending is the right outcome. But there is a difference between a marriage that ends because it genuinely should and a marriage that ends because the difficulty of a hard season was mistaken for evidence that the marriage itself was wrong. People leave during winters that would have become springs.

The question I am most often asked by younger people who know about our marriage is some version of: "What is the secret?" I have two answers.

The first is: marry your best friend. Not the most impressive person you know. Not the most attractive person available at the time you are ready to marry. Your best friend. The person you would call if something wonderful happened. The person you would call if something terrible happened. The person who knows the version of you that exists when no one is performing for anyone, and who shows up anyway.

A marriage built on friendship has a resource that a marriage built on other things does not: when the romance is complicated, when the circumstances are hard, when the season is a winter rather than a spring, the friendship is still there. It sustains things that other foundations cannot sustain.

The second answer is: work through the differences. Not around them. Not by accumulating them in a place where they are quietly stored and periodically retrieved. Through them. This requires the willingness to have the conversation that is hard to have, to say the thing that is hard to say, to hear the thing that is hard to hear, and to keep going after all of that has happened.

My wife and I are approaching fifty years. Thirty of them were happy, as I tell people, and they laugh, and what I mean is: all fifty of them were real. The happy ones were genuinely happy. The difficult ones were genuinely difficult. Working through the difficult ones is what produced the happy ones, which is the part of the story that the joke does not quite carry, but that I hope the life does.

The sun came up on the hard mornings, too. It always did. We were still there when it came up, which is the part that mattered.

If you want happiness in marriage, marry your best friend. Work through the differences rather than around them. Trust that the good seasons are coming, because they are. And when the hard season arrives, which it will, remember that seasons end. The sun will come up tomorrow. It came up on every difficult day of a marriage that is approaching fifty years, and I would not trade a single one of them, including the twenty.

Chapter 12

PURPOSE

Purpose is the answer to the question the alarm clock asks every morning: why get up? When the answer is clear and compelling, the alarm is almost unnecessary. When the answer is absent or uncertain, even the most comfortable life can feel strangely hollow.

The research on purpose is consistent and striking. People who have a strong sense of why they get up in the morning live longer on average, recover more quickly from illness and setbacks, and report significantly higher levels of life satisfaction than those who do not. Purpose is not a luxury available only to people whose work happens to be meaningful. It is a fundamental human need, as real as food and sleep, and just as consequential when it is missing.

What makes the stories in this chapter worth examining together is that none of them follow the path we are usually told purpose takes. Robert did not find his teaching vocation until he was sixty-one, after the career he planned was taken from him. Claire did not abandon her marketing role for something purer. She found a room where she was mostly alive and visited it regularly enough to remember who she was. These stories were about a question, asked persistently enough, finally receiving an honest answer.

Purpose does not retire on schedule. It is available at every age and at every stage, including and especially the ones that feel like endings.

The Retired Adviser Who Became a Teacher

The door that closes is rarely the last door. This is one of those things that is easy to say and genuinely difficult to believe when you are standing in front of the closed one. The gap between the intellectual understanding that other opportunities exist and the lived experience of having the option you had planned on disappear is wider than most people expect. What fills that gap, most of the time, is not wisdom. It is grief. And grief has its own timeline, which rarely cooperates with the urgency we feel to get on with things.

Robert's story is not a story about bouncing back quickly. It is a story about what becomes visible when you stop staring at the door that closed long enough to notice what else is in the room.

Situation

Robert spent thirty-one years in financial services. He built a career methodically, client by client, year by year, and had arrived at the final stretch with every intention of finishing on his own terms. He did not finish on his own terms.

At sixty-one, with retirement close enough to taste, he was let go. The language was careful and corporate, but the meaning was plain. The timing was not accidental. He understood that. The company had done the math, and he was on the wrong side of it.

Turning Point

His daughter called one evening and mentioned, almost as an aside, that his grandson would soon be living four hours closer. Robert drove out the following weekend and watched his grandson struggle through a page of math homework at the kitchen table.

He sat down next to him and walked him through it. Forty minutes later, the homework was done, and the boy was asking questions that went three pages beyond the assignment.

On the drive home, Robert made two decisions. He would relocate. And he would look into what it took to teach high school mathematics. He was hired by a public high school the following fall.

Lesson

Robert spent three decades helping people manage money. What he discovered in a high school classroom was that he had always been in the business of the long view. The instrument had simply changed. The door that closed on a Tuesday afternoon in a corporate office was not the last door. It was the one that needed to close before he would bother looking for the next one.

What Robert's students received that most of their other teachers could not offer was not just mathematical knowledge. It was the visible example of a man who had been genuinely useful in a demanding professional context, who had been knocked off the path he intended, and who had found, at sixty-one, that his best teaching was still ahead of him. That example teaches something no curriculum delivers: that it is not too late, that beginning again is not the same as failing, and that the person standing at the front of the room has been somewhere real and chosen to come back to them.

There is a version of this story available to most people who have arrived at a closed door later in their career. It does not require teaching high school mathematics. It requires only the willingness to ask, honestly, what the grandson at the kitchen table represents in your own life. Where is the thing that lights you up the way that homework lit Robert up? Whatever it is, the path to it is probably not designed for someone in a hurry. Take it anyway.

The Woman Who Stopped Performing

Situation

For nineteen years, Claire had been very good at a job she stopped caring about somewhere around year eleven.

She was a senior marketing director for a consumer goods company, the kind of role that reads impressively on a resume and requires, in practice, an enormous amount of energy directed at things that feel, in the quiet hours, not entirely worth the energy. She was skilled at it. She was recognized for it. She received the reviews, the raises, and the invitations to present at the annual leadership summit that served as the organization's annual reminder to its people that the organization valued them.

She valued the salary. She was honest enough to admit that to herself, if to no one else. What she stopped being honest about, for longer than she could precisely identify, was everything else.

The work had not always felt hollow. There had been a time, early in the role, when the problems were genuinely interesting, and the team was genuinely hers, and the day had a forward momentum that felt like meaning. She confused that feeling with the job itself. What she eventually understood was that the feeling had come from learning, from building, from the particular aliveness of someone doing something for the first time and discovering they were good at it. The job hadn't changed. She had. She had mastered it, and mastery without growth is its own kind of trap.

She did not know this yet when she signed up to volunteer at her daughter's school on a Thursday afternoon in October.

She signed up because her daughter asked, and because she had said no to enough school things that the yes felt overdue.

Turning Point

The assignment was to help a group of eighth graders work through a project on local businesses: what they sold, who their customers were, how they made decisions about what to stock and what to drop. The teacher had framed it as a social studies exercise. Claire looked at it and saw a marketing problem.

She sat down with a table of thirteen-year-olds who were, by their own cheerful admission, entirely uninterested in the assignment, and she started asking questions. Not the worksheet questions. Real ones. Why do you think that store puts the candy by the register? Who do you think they're trying to sell to? If you were trying to get someone your age to notice something on a shelf, what would you do?

The table woke up.

For the next ninety minutes, Claire forgot entirely that she had a four o'clock call she was going to have to reschedule, a campaign brief due by Friday, and a director who had sent three follow-up emails on a thread she had been avoiding for two weeks. She was fully present in a way she had not been in a professional context in longer than she could remember, not because the stakes were high but because the people across the table were genuinely curious and she was the person who could meet that curiosity with something real.

She drove home and sat in the parking garage for a few minutes before going inside.

Something happened in that classroom that had not happened at work in years. She mattered in a way that she could feel rather than measure.

Lesson

Claire did not quit her job the next morning. Life is rarely that clean, and she was practical enough to understand that a Thursday afternoon in an eighth-grade classroom is not a career plan.

But she started paying attention to what the afternoon told her, and what it told her was not complicated: she wanted to teach. Not necessarily in a school, not necessarily full-time, not necessarily in any form she could yet specify. But the particular experience of watching someone understand something for the first time, because of something she offered, was the closest thing to purpose she felt in a decade.

Over the following two years, she built a parallel track alongside her marketing career, developing a workshop curriculum for small business owners on brand positioning and customer psychology. She taught it on weekends at first, then through a local chamber of commerce, then at a community college that asked her to formalize it into a continuing education course.

She still works in marketing. She may always work in marketing. But she is no longer only working in marketing, and the person who shows up to the four o'clock call on Thursdays is visibly different from the one who was avoiding the thread two years ago. She has somewhere else to put her best energy, and having somewhere else to put it turns out to make everything else better.

Purpose, it turns out, does not always require a complete reinvention. Sometimes it only requires finding the one room where you are most alive, and making sure you spend enough time in it to remember who you actually are.

Claire found hers in a school on a Thursday afternoon, with a table of thirteen-year-olds who wanted to know why the candy was by the register.

She has been answering that question, in one form or another, ever since.

Chapter 13

GRATITUDE

There is a version of gratitude that everyone understands and almost no one finds particularly useful: the gratitude that arrives automatically when things are going well. You get the news you hoped for. You finish a difficult project. Something good happens, and you feel grateful. This version of gratitude is real and worth noticing. But it is not what this chapter is about.

This chapter is about the other kind. The gratitude that has to be chosen when things are not going well. The deliberate act of looking at what remains after something has been taken. The discipline of directing attention toward what is still present rather than measuring the distance to what is gone. This kind of gratitude is not a mood. It is a practice, and like all practices, it produces results that are directly proportional to the consistency with which it is applied.

The two stories here approach this from different directions. Martin lost nearly everything material and found, in a dark apartment in the middle of the night, that what remained was more than he had been seeing. My brother-in-law gained nearly everything material and discovered that what he lost was the one thing the money could not replace. Together, they make the same point from opposite ends: happiness is not determined by the inventory of what we have. It is determined by the attention we pay to what matters.

Gratitude is the most underestimated driver of happiness. It is also one of the most researched. Study after study finds that people who practice gratitude consistently, not as a feeling they wait for but as a discipline they choose, report higher levels of well-being, stronger relationships, and greater resilience than those who do not.

The keyword is practice. Gratitude is not a mood. It is a decision about where to direct attention.

The challenge is that gratitude is hardest to access precisely when it is most needed. When life is going well, gratitude feels natural and effortless. When life has taken something from us, or several things, gratitude feels like a small and inadequate response to a large and concrete loss. The people who learned to practice it through difficulty are not people who found a way to pretend the losses were acceptable. They are people who have learned to hold both things at once: the loss is real, and so is what remains. The inventory of what is gone matters. So does the inventory of what is still here.

The Person Who Lost Everything

It is easy to be grateful when nothing has been taken from you. The practice that actually matters, the one that shapes how a life feels from the inside, is the gratitude that chooses to look at what remains after the taking. Martin did not discover this through philosophy, practice, or intention. He discovered it at two in the morning on a secondhand couch, in the dark, with a dog on the floor and a son who had nowhere better to be.

Situation

By any reasonable measure, Martin had built a good life. Twenty-two years growing a regional logistics company from a borrowed office into an operation with forty employees. A home he renovated himself. A wife of nineteen years. Two teenage sons. A dog that met him at the door every evening as though his arrival was the finest development in recorded history.

He was not a man who took things for granted. He said grace before dinner. He coached youth baseball for eleven years. He called his mother on Sundays.

And then, in the span of fourteen months, the structure came down. The company lost its two largest contracts. He filed for bankruptcy. His marriage did not survive the collapse. He moved into a two-bedroom apartment and learned, at fifty-three, how to cook for one.

Turning Point

Eight months after the divorce, his younger son came to spend a weekend. They made sandwiches for dinner. They watched a game. They fell asleep on opposite ends of the couch.

At some point in the middle of the night, Martin woke up and his son was still there, asleep, taking up more of the couch than was strictly necessary. The dog was on the floor between them, twitching through some private dream.

Martin sat for a long while in the dark, not thinking about the company or the house or the marriage. He was thinking about the fact that his son had chosen to spend a Saturday night on a secondhand couch in a two-bedroom apartment when he could have been anywhere else.

And something shifted. Not dramatically. Just a quiet rearrangement, like furniture moved a few inches in a room that suddenly felt larger. He lost a great deal. He had not lost everything.

Lesson

Gratitude is not something you feel when life is good. Anyone can manage that. Gratitude, the real kind, is something you practice when life has taken things from you, and you choose to look at what's left rather than measure the distance to what's gone.

Perspective gained through loss is not silver-lining thinking. It does not require pretending the loss was acceptable. It only requires the willingness, in a quiet moment in the dark, to look at the couch instead of the empty space where the house used to be.

What is still here? For most of us, the honest answer is more than we think.

Martin would go on to lead the men's group he joined the following year, which is its own kind of lesson. The man who had nothing left to give, sitting in a dark apartment with a dog and a son and a secondhand couch, became the man other men came to when they needed someone who had been through something and made it back. His losses did not disqualify him from leading. They qualified him. The credibility he had in that room came from the fact that he had sat in the dark and done the inventory and found more than he expected. He could say that because he lived it, and the men in that room knew the difference between someone who lived it and someone who was reciting it from a book.

The inventory of what remains is always worth taking. The act of taking it, done honestly and without the instinct to minimize what was lost or exaggerate what was left, is itself a form of resilience. It is the refusal to let the accounting of loss be the only accounting. Martin lost a company. He lost a marriage. He lost a house. He kept two sons, a dog, a brother, his health, his name, and the capacity to start again. That last one turned out to be worth more than everything he had lost combined.

The Man Who Had Everything but Was Miserable

Money occupies a complicated place in conversations about happiness. The research suggests that it matters up to the point that financial security removes a category of stress that genuinely corrodes wellbeing, but that beyond a certain threshold, additional wealth adds very little to how happy a person actually feels. Most people, when told this, nod in agreement and then continue organizing their lives as though the opposite were true.

My brother-in-law's story does not argue that money is meaningless. It argues something more specific and more sobering: that money acquired after the thing that gave your life its meaning is already gone cannot replace what is gone. It can only make the absence more visible.

Situation

My brother-in-law lived a simple life, and for a long time, a genuinely happy one. He didn't date much growing up and came to marriage through a chance encounter with a woman a few years older than him, divorced, with two young children whose biological father walked away. He stepped into the role of father to those children as naturally as if he had been there from the beginning. They were happy. I watched it and knew it to be true.

Then, in the middle of all of it, a lottery ticket was won.

He pooled money with two business associates for a routine Friday afternoon purchase. The ticket was a winner: $12 million. After taxes, well over two million dollars came to a man who spent his entire life in a small town where that sum made him, overnight, one of the wealthiest people anyone around him knew.

Turning Point

The money could not save his wife, whose health had been failing for nearly twenty years of their marriage. And it made him visible to people who did not have his best interests at heart. The investments he was drawn into turned out to be fraudulent. The money that was supposed to represent security was systematically taken from him by people he trusted.

And then his wife died.

The man who organized his entire life around her was now wealthy by every external measure and devastated in every way that actually mattered. The depression that followed was deep. He questioned openly whether he wanted to continue living without her. He tried. I want to say that clearly because it is true and it matters. But the two years that followed her death were defined by the choices of a man who lost the person who gave his choices meaning. He died at forty-six years old.

Lesson

I think about him when people talk about money and happiness as though the relationship between them is straightforward. He could have written the book on why it isn't.

The happiest years of his life were the ones with the least money, the years when he was raising children that weren't biologically his, caring for a wife whose health was failing, living quietly in a small town where nobody particularly noticed him. He was not missing anything during those years that the lottery ticket later provided. He was full. The fullness came from her, from the children, from the specific weight of being needed by people who loved him back.

If there is a single question worth asking today, it is this: if everything you have accumulated disappeared tomorrow, what would you still have that made the whole thing worth it? If you can answer that question quickly and without hesitation, you are wealthier than you know.

I share this story with care because it belongs to a real person I loved, and it does not have a redemptive ending. He did not find his way back. The depression was too deep and the losses too total, and the two years that followed her death moved in a direction that nothing seemed to interrupt. He died at forty-six, and I think about him still.

What I carry from his life, and what I offer here, is not a warning about money. It is a reminder about what money cannot carry. He had known exactly what gave his life its weight: her, the children, the simple dignity of being needed by people who loved him back. He had lived that knowledge faithfully for twenty years. The tragedy is not that he won the lottery. The tragedy is that the lottery arrived after the one thing irreplaceable was already slipping away, and then was gone, and no amount of anything could answer the question of what to do next.

Know what yours is. Tend it accordingly. The rest is arithmetic.

Chapter 14

RESILIENCE

Resilience is the quality that makes everything else possible. Without it, perspective collapses under pressure. Relationships cannot survive the weight of genuine hardship. Purpose fades when the circumstances that supported it change. Gratitude becomes impossible in the face of accumulating loss. Resilience is the foundation on which the other drivers rest, and it is the one that matters most when the others are being tested.

The difficulty with resilience is that it cannot be developed in comfortable conditions. It requires the thing it is designed to respond to: difficulty. This means that every setback, every loss, every period of genuine struggle is simultaneously an opportunity to build the quality that will make the next one more survivable. This is not a comforting thought in the middle of the difficulty. It becomes one in retrospect, which is where resilience tends to reveal itself most clearly.

The stories in this chapter approach that truth from two very different directions.

One is public and witnessed by millions. Jack Hughes, bloodied and missing teeth in the third period of an Olympic gold medal game, picked himself up and scored the overtime winner to end a forty-six-year American drought. That version of resilience is visible, dramatic, and immediately legible. You can see it on a screen. You can point to the moment and say: There. That is what it looks like.

The other is private and witnessed by almost no one. A seven-year-old boy in an empty church parking lot on a Saturday morning, alone after his father drove away, falling off a bicycle and getting back up. Again, and again. Until he could ride. What I did not know then, and would not understand until years later, is that he was not simply fighting discouragement or the ordinary difficulty of learning something new. He was fighting a neurological condition he had been born with, and that no one had yet found. The obstacle was invisible. He overcame it anyway.

That second story is the one I find more instructive. Not because public resilience is less real, but because most of us will face the version that happens in parking lots rather than on Olympic ice. The version where no one is watching. The version where we do not fully understand what we are up against. The version where the only witness to the breakthrough is us.

Resilience is not the absence of struggle. It is the decision, made repeatedly and often in the absence of any certainty that it will matter, to keep going anyway. It is not a trait that some people have and others lack. It is a practice, available to anyone willing to choose it, including a seven-year-old boy who had every reason to stay down and kept getting up instead.

The Parking Lot

Situation

My youngest son was a big kid from the day he arrived in the world, and size, it turns out, has its complications.

He was larger than most of his friends, and the gap showed up in unexpected places. One of them was a bicycle. The bikes available to children his age were built for children considerably smaller than him, and his shoe size in particular made the mechanics of pedaling genuinely difficult in a way that had nothing to do with effort or coordination. The pedals were too close together, the geometry was wrong, and no amount of trying seemed to close the gap between where he was and where he needed to be.

He tried anyway. His older brother helped. I helped. He fell. He got up. He fell again.

I watched this repeat itself over months and eventually stopped bringing it up, because watching him fail was harder than I had expected it to be, and I could not find a way to help him that actually helped.

What made it harder was the door.

Friends would knock, bikes at the ready, asking if he wanted to come ride. He would make excuses. Different excuses on different days, carefully chosen to avoid the real answer. He was too embarrassed to say what the real answer was, and I was too sad watching it to push the conversation toward the truth. We had quietly, without ever saying so directly, given up.

Turning Point

He was about seven years old when he came to me on a Saturday morning and said he wanted to try one more time. I did not want to say yes. I knew what one more time looked like. I had watched it enough times to have the whole sequence memorized: the positioning, the wobble, the fall, the expression on his face afterward that he was working so hard to keep neutral. I did not want to see that expression again.

He insisted.

I loaded the bike into the SUV and drove to the parking lot of our church, which was empty on a Saturday morning and far enough from the neighborhood that his friends were unlikely to see. We had chosen the location without saying why we had chosen it. We both knew.

I held the bike. He positioned himself. He fell, the same way he had fallen before, and we worked through it together for a while, and then something happened that I am not proud of and that I have thought about many times since.

I could not face it.

Not his failure. Mine. The helplessness of a father who wanted to fix something he could not fix, who had watched this child absorb this particular disappointment more times than either of them should have had to, and who in that moment had nothing useful left to offer.

I told him I needed to get gas. That I would be back soon. I drove away.

Turning Point

About thirty seconds down the road, I understood what I had done. I had left a seven-year-old boy alone in a parking lot with a bicycle because watching him try and fail had become more than I could carry. The worry arrived immediately; what if he fell and hurt himself, what if something happened, what kind of father leaves and goes to get gas; and underneath the worry was the recognition that I had let my own feelings make the decision rather than his needs.

I got gas. I drove back.

As I turned into the parking lot, I saw him standing next to the bicycle. He waved.

Then he got on the bike and rode it around the parking lot.

I sat in the car for a moment before I got out, because I needed a moment. He was riding. Not perfectly, not with the easy confidence of kids who had been doing it for years, but riding. Moving under his own power, in circles, in an empty church parking lot on a Saturday morning, with no one watching except his father through a windshield.

When I got out of the car, I saw his pants. They were torn at both knees. His hands had dried blood on them from where he had caught himself falling. He had not stopped when I left. He had kept going, alone, falling and getting up, falling and getting up, until the thing that had been impossible was no longer impossible.

We loaded the bike into the SUV. On the drive home, he was quiet for a moment, and then he said: "Dad, this is the happiest day of my life."

I thought I understood that story for years. I thought it was about persistence, about a child who refused to quit, about the morning when determination finally outran failure. I told it that way in my own mind, as a father does with stories that matter to him, shaping them over time into something he can carry without too much weight.

I did not understand it fully until he was in high school.

He had always had a large head. This was simply a fact about him, the way some people are tall or left-handed, something you note and then stop noticing because it is just part of who the person is. When he started playing football, we discovered that standard helmets would not fit him. We had a helmet custom-made; the kind built for players on the Dallas Cowboys roster. His teammates found this impressive. We found it practical. We did not yet understand what it meant.

He started having headaches. Persistent ones, the kind that do not respond the way ordinary headaches respond. My wife was not satisfied with the first explanations or the second ones. She took him to specialist after specialist, following a thread that conventional medicine kept suggesting was not there, until one physician finally found what the others had missed.

A cyst. Congenital, meaning he had been born with it. The size of an orange. Sitting on his brain.

His skull had stopped growing while the cyst had not, and the result was pressure that had been building quietly for his entire life. The large head was not incidental. It was the skull accommodating what was inside it. The headaches were not mysterious. They were the pressure announcing itself loudly enough that it could no longer be ignored.

He went through microsurgery to relieve it. The procedure was delicate in the way that brain surgery is always delicate, and the recovery was its own kind of difficulty. When it was done and he had come through it, I asked him whether he felt any different.

He said he did. He said he had never been able to stand up straight before. And now he could.

I stood there for a moment with that.

He had never been able to stand up straight. For his entire childhood, through every sport and every classroom and every ordinary day of moving through the world, he had been compensating for something he did not know was there, something none of us knew was there, because it had always been there and therefore seemed like simply how things were.

And then I thought about the parking lot.

It was not his shoe size that had made the bicycle so difficult. It was not the geometry of a child's bike built for a smaller child. It was not effort, or coordination, or the gap between wanting something and being able to do it.

It was balance.

A cyst the size of an orange pressing on a brain does things to a person's ability to balance. A seven-year-old boy with that cyst, in a church parking lot on a Saturday morning, alone after his father had driven away to get gas, was not fighting discouragement or embarrassment or the simple difficulty of learning to ride a bike.

He was fighting against a neurological condition that made balance physiologically compromised, that had been present since before he was born, that no one had yet identified, and that would not be found for years.

And he won.

He fell and got up, fell and got up, in an empty parking lot with no one watching and torn pants and bleeding hands, and he figured out how to ride a bicycle despite a condition that had every right to make that impossible, because he had decided that morning that he wanted to try one more time.

The happiest day of his life.

Lesson

I have told the parking lot story before, as a story about persistence. It is still that. But knowing what I know now, it is also something more specific and more remarkable.

Most resilience is built against visible obstacles. The setback you can name, the difficulty you can describe, the opponent you can see clearly enough to fight. The stories we tell about resilience tend to feature that kind of clarity: here is what stood in the way, here is what it cost to get past it, here is what was waiting on the other side.

My son's resilience was built against something he could not name, could not see, and would not understand for years. He did not know he was compensating for a cyst when he kept trying to ride the bike. He did not know his balance was compromised by something structural rather than something correctable with practice. He knew only that this thing his friends did easily was not easy for him, and that he was going to keep trying until it was.

That is a different kind of determination than the ordinary kind. The ordinary kind knows what it is fighting. His kind fought in the dark, without a diagnosis, without an explanation, and without any way to know whether the effort was worth continuing or whether the obstacle was simply permanent.

He continued anyway.

When the surgery was over and he stood up straight for the first time in his life, that was its own form of resilience. But the parking lot happened before any of that. The parking lot happened when the obstacle was invisible and unnamed, and the only thing he had to work with was the refusal to accept that the falling was the final answer.

I was not there for the moment he figured it out. I had driven away.

He did not need me there. That is the thing I have come to understand, slowly and with some difficulty, about the children we raise and the obstacles we cannot fix for them. They do not always need us present for the breakthrough. Sometimes they need us to trust that the breakthrough is coming, and to have given them enough, across enough ordinary days, that they have what they need to reach it alone.

He reached it alone. In a parking lot. With torn pants and a cyst on his brain the size of an orange, and not a single person watching.

The happiest day of his life. I believe him.

The Athlete Who Failed Before Winning

Sports offer us compressed, visible versions of the human experiences that play out more slowly and less dramatically in ordinary life. The injury that sidelines a season. The slump that makes a talented person question whether they were ever as good as they thought. The moment in overtime when everything comes down to one play, and the person best positioned to make it is the one who has spent the past several months looking like a question mark.

We watch sports in part because we recognize ourselves in these stories, even when we have never laced up skates or touched a puck. The forty-six-year drought is someone's career plateau. The missed twenty-one games are someone's lost quarter. The high stick that costs you several teeth in the third period of the most important game of your life is whatever your version of that moment is. Most of us have had one. The question is the same regardless of the sport.

Situation

For forty-six years, American men's hockey lived in the shadow of a single February night in 1980: a group of college kids in Lake Placid who beat the Soviet Union and made a nation stop breathing. Every American team that followed carried that legacy into every tournament and came home without adding to it.

Jack Hughes arrived at the 2026 Milan Olympics as one of America's brightest stars, and one of its most quietly doubted. Coming into the Games, he missed twenty-one games with his NHL club and managed only one goal in his last eighteen. He was talented enough to be on the roster and struggling enough that questions followed him onto the ice.

Late in the gold medal game against Canada, Hughes took a high stick to the face. He was bloodied and lost several front teeth. He picked his teeth up off the ice and never missed a shift.

Turning Point

One minute and forty-one seconds into overtime, Hughes received a pass from Zach Werenski and slipped the puck between the goaltender's legs to seal a 2-1 American victory, ending a forty-six-year drought.

Through a bloodied mouth, he praised not himself but his teammates: "USA Hockey brotherhood means so much. Look at these guys. We're such a team."

And when the celebration began, the team took the ice carrying the jersey of their late teammate Johnny Gaudreau, killed by a drunk driver in 2024 on the eve of his sister's wedding. The gold medal belonged to all of them, including the one who never got to skate for it.

Lesson

Jack Hughes didn't arrive in Milan as a sure thing. He arrived as a question mark, injured, in a slump, carrying the weight of what the prior months had cost him. What he demonstrated in overtime, toothless and bloodied, was the essential truth about resilience: it is not the absence of struggle. It is the decision to keep skating through it.

Every person moving through a difficult season faces the same choice Hughes faced in that third period: stay on the bench and protect yourself or get back out there and be ready when the puck finds you.

Forty-six years of waiting ended not with a miracle, but with a man who had every reason to be diminished and refused to be. The goal itself took less than two seconds. The preparation for it took a lifetime.

The detail that stays with me is not the goal. It is the teeth. Hughes picked his teeth up off the ice and went back to the bench and kept playing. He did not ask to come out. He did not use the injury as cover for a cautious approach in overtime. He was bloodied and missing pieces of himself, and he was still, when the puck found him one minute and forty-one seconds into the extra period, ready. That is what preparation for the big moment actually looks like. Not the dramatic speech before the game. Not the confident pre-game warmup. The decision, made in the middle of actual pain, to stay in.

The team carrying Johnny Gaudreau's jersey onto the ice adds another dimension that the individual story alone cannot carry. Resilience is not only personal. It is collective. The jersey was a statement about what that team was playing for, which was larger than any individual on it. When a group of people share a loss and choose to carry it together rather than be diminished by it, something happens to the group's capacity that individual resilience alone cannot produce. They become capable of more than the sum of their parts, not despite the loss, but partly because of what carrying it together required of them.

Two stories. One parking lot, one Olympic ice rink. One witnessed by a father through a windshield; one watched by millions around the world. The principle running through both of them is identical: the obstacle does not determine the outcome. The decision to keep going does.

Your version of this chapter may look nothing like either of these. It may be quieter, more private, entirely your own. But somewhere in your life, there is a parking lot. A moment when the thing you were trying to do refused to cooperate, when the people around you could not fix it, when the only resource you had left was the willingness to try one more time.

That willingness is enough. It has always been enough.

The sun came up the next morning after every one of those attempts. It will come up after yours.

Chapter 15

HUMOR AND LIGHTHEARTEDNESS

One of the missing pieces in many conversations about happiness is humor. Not as denial. Not as performance. Not as a policy of pretending everything is fine. Real laughter does something else. It interrupts the accumulation of unrelieved anxiety and reminds us that even in serious seasons, fear does not have to have the whole room to itself.

The Waiting Room That Wasn't

Situation

Nobody had ever described the fourth-floor oncology waiting room at St. Augustine Medical Center as a place where people laughed.

It was a well-designed room, as waiting rooms in serious medical facilities go. Good lighting. Comfortable chairs. A small table with magazines that were six months out of date, which is the universal standard for medical waiting room magazines and which no one has ever successfully explained. There was a television mounted in the corner, turned to a cable news channel with the sound off, which was either a mercy or an oversight depending on your perspective.

People came to this room carrying the specific weight that people carry when the news they are waiting for is the kind that reorganizes everything. They sat with their phones or with their hands or with the middle distance, and they were quiet in the way that people are quiet when the silence feels appropriate to the circumstances.

And then, one Tuesday morning in March, a man named Bernard sat down next to a woman named Octavia, and everything changed.

Bernard was sixty-seven years old, a retired high school band director from a small city in Georgia, and he had been coming to the fourth floor waiting room every three weeks for four months while his wife underwent treatment for breast cancer. He was not, by temperament, a gloomy man. He had spent thirty-one years directing teenagers through musical pieces they were not yet technically qualified to play, which requires a specific variety of optimism that either breaks a person or becomes permanent, and in Bernard's case, had become permanent.

He had been quiet in the waiting room for the first two months because the room was quiet and he respected what the room seemed to be asking of him. But he noticed, over those two months, something that troubled him in a way he had gradually decided he was not going to ignore.

The people in this room were suffering twice.

They were suffering the obvious way, the way that brought them here: the illness and the treatment and the uncertainty and the love directed at someone going through something frightening. That suffering was real and Bernard did not minimize it.

But they were also suffering the way people suffer when they sit alone with their fear for hours at a time with nothing to interrupt it. The waiting room had become, through no one's particular fault, a container for unrelieved anxiety. People arrived already frightened and left more frightened than when they came, because the room had given the fear four hours of uninterrupted time to work with.

Bernard, who spent thirty-one years refusing to let a room full of people stay in a bad place when he had any ability to change it, decided he was done being quiet.

Turning Point

He sat down next to Octavia, who was sixty-one, a retired elementary school librarian from the same city who had been coming to the fourth floor for six weeks while her husband received treatment for lymphoma. She had a book open in her lap that she had not been reading for forty minutes.

Bernard looked at the book. It was a novel with a sailboat on the cover.

"Any good?" he said.

Octavia looked up with the mild wariness of someone not certain what was being initiated. "I genuinely have no idea," she said. "I've read the same paragraph eleven times."

Bernard nodded. "What paragraph?"

She looked down. "The sea was calm that morning, which Geoffrey had learned to distrust."

Bernard considered this. "Geoffrey sounds like a man with experience."

Something crossed Octavia's face that was almost a smile. "He really does."

"What do you think happened to Geoffrey?"

"I think Geoffrey is about to have a very bad day," Octavia said, "and is the only person in the vicinity who knows it."

Bernard laughed. An actual laugh, not the polite kind. Octavia laughed with him, and the laugh was, by her own later description, the first one she had produced in six weeks that felt like it came from somewhere real rather than somewhere performed.

The woman across the room looked up from her phone. Bernard had not planned what happened next, or at least not in any formal sense. What he had planned was to stop being quiet, and the rest followed from that.

He and Octavia talked about Geoffrey and his doomed calm sea for a few minutes, and then about the books they had each been meaning to read for years and had never read, and then about the particular comedy of medical waiting rooms and the magazines that were always six months out of date, which led to a brief and genuinely funny exchange about what was in those magazines that made no one want to take them home, which led to a theory from Bernard that the magazines were deliberately chosen to be undesirable as a theft deterrent, which led to a discussion of what a magazine would have to contain to be worth stealing from an oncology waiting room.

The woman across the room, whose name was Shirley, had put her phone in her bag.

A man in the corner named Devaughn, who had been staring at the muted cable news with the expression of someone watching a language he did not speak, had turned his chair slightly toward the conversation.

Within twenty minutes, without any formal invitation being extended, six people in the fourth-floor oncology waiting room were talking to each other. Not about their diagnoses, not about their fear, not about the thing that had brought them to this particular room on this particular Tuesday. About Geoffrey and his calm sea. About magazine theft deterrence strategy. About Bernard's thirty-one years of trying to get teenagers to play

Beethoven in tune, which produced three stories of increasing absurdity that had Shirley laughing so hard she had to put her hand over her mouth.

The room had not changed. The lighting was the same. The chairs were the same. The six-month-old magazines were still on the table. The television was still showing cable news with the sound off.

What had changed was the air.

A nurse named Helen, who worked the fourth floor for nine years and who had seen the waiting room in many configurations, stopped at the doorway at one point during the morning and looked in at six people who were, against all the room's apparent intentions, laughing.

She stood there for a moment. Then she went and found two of her colleagues and brought them to the doorway.

"Look at that," she said.

They looked.

"Bernard?" one of them said, who recognized him from four months of Tuesday visits.

"Bernard," Helen confirmed.

She made a decision, standing at that doorway, that she had been thinking about making for two years. She went to the supply room and came back with a table, which she set up near the chairs. Then she went to the break room and came back with a coffee maker, a box of tea bags, and a plate of cookies that had been brought in by someone's family that morning and that were sitting on the counter waiting for a purpose.

She set them on the table.

"These are for you," she said to the room, to no one in particular. "We should have done this a long time ago."

Bernard looked at the cookies and then at Helen and then back at the cookies.

"Are these a theft deterrent," he said, "or are we allowed to eat them?"

Helen laughed so hard she had to hold onto the doorframe.

Bernard became, over the following months, a fixture of the fourth floor waiting room in a way that the staff came to appreciate and the other patients came to rely on. He was not cheerful in the hollow, performance-art way of someone who has decided that positivity is a policy. He was warm, genuinely funny, and honest in the way that people who have earned their laughter through genuine difficulty are honest. He did not pretend the room was not what it was. He simply refused to let it be only what it was.

His wife completed her treatment successfully in June. The last Tuesday, he came to the waiting room, and Octavia was there, and Devaughn, and Shirley, and several people he had met in the preceding months. Helen brought a cake.

There were no speeches. Nobody said anything particularly significant. They ate cake in an oncology waiting room on a Tuesday morning, and they laughed, and when Bernard stood up to leave for the last time, the room felt the loss of him before he was through the door.

He had not changed anyone's diagnosis. He had not accelerated anyone's treatment or improved anyone's prognosis or solved any of the medical problems that had brought twelve strangers to a room on the fourth floor of a hospital.

What he had done was refuse to let the fear have the room to itself. That turned out to matter more than anyone had expected.

Octavia's husband completed his treatment in August. She went back to the fourth floor once, a few months later, not as a patient's family member but simply to visit Helen, who had kept the coffee table stocked every Tuesday since March.

She sat for a while in the room where she had first laughed in six weeks, in the chair where Bernard had asked about Geoffrey and his calm sea, and she thought about what the laughter had done for her during those months.

It had not removed the fear. Nothing removed the fear. The fear was present and real and appropriate to the circumstances.

What the laughter had done was prevent the fear from being the only thing present. It had shared the room with something else, something human and warm and genuinely funny, and the sharing had made the fear more manageable. Not smaller, exactly. More proportionate. Held in a context that included other things alongside it, rather than occupying the whole space alone.

She had read somewhere that it is physiologically difficult to sustain anxiety at full intensity while laughing. She did not know whether the science was rigorous. She knew it was true. She had experienced it every Tuesday morning for six weeks, in a waiting room where a retired band director had refused to be quiet, and the experience had been one of the most important of her adult life.

Not because the laughter solved anything.

Because it reminded her, reliably and repeatedly, that the situation she was in was not the entirety of the world. That joy and sorrow could occupy the same room. That the cable news could be on mute in the corner and Geoffrey could still be heading into rough water and the cookies could still be worth eating and the people around her were still capable of laughing, which meant she was still capable of laughing, which meant something she had not been able to name was still intact.

Bernard had known this for thirty-one years of directing teenagers through music they were not quite ready to play. The room full of people who could not quite get Beethoven in tune was always closer to something beautiful than it appeared. You just had to refuse to let it be only what it was.

The fourth floor waiting room was the same. Every room is.

The Lesson

Bernard did not walk into that waiting room with a philosophy. He walked in with a temperament, the particular disposition of someone who spent a career refusing to let a room full of people stay in a bad place when he had any ability to change it. The philosophy arrived afterward, when other people tried to explain what he had done and why it mattered.

What he understood, practically and without needing to articulate it, is the same thing the research on humor and well-being consistently finds: laughter is not the opposite of seriousness. It does not trivialize difficulty or deny the reality of painful circumstances. It interrupts the accumulation of unrelieved anxiety, which, left alone in a room for hours at a time, produces a kind of suffering that is distinct from and additional to the suffering that brought you there.

You cannot laugh and worry at full intensity simultaneously. This is not a motivational claim. It is a physiological one. And in a room where the worrying is legitimate and the circumstances are genuinely serious, the temporary interruption of that physiological state is not an escape from the difficulty. It is a form of maintenance. It keeps people functional, present, and connected to each other in a way that unrelieved dread does not.

Bernard gave twelve strangers on a Tuesday morning in March a place to put something other than their fear. They brought the fear anyway. They always would. But they also brought the laughter, and the laughter shared the room with the fear, and the sharing made both the fear and the room more bearable than either would have been alone.

That is what humor does when it is genuine. Not performed, not deployed as a policy, not forced into spaces where it does not belong. When it arrives naturally, from a person who is actually funny and actually warm and actually willing to be human in a room that asks everyone to be only afraid, it changes the air.

Geoffrey never had a good day, as it turned out. The sea that was calm that morning was not calm by afternoon, and things went badly for him in ways that Octavia eventually read about, weeks later, when she finally got past that paragraph.

She found it enormously funny that she spent six weeks in an oncology waiting room laughing about a man whose problems were entirely fictional.

Bernard, when she told him, said that was probably the point. She thought he was right.

The Department That Laughed

Situation

Nobody ever wanted to transfer into Howard Briggs's department.

This was not because Howard was a bad manager. By most measurable standards, he was a good one: fair, organized, technically competent, genuinely invested in developing his people. The metrics were solid. The reviews were positive. HR had no file on Howard Briggs that contained anything concerning.

The reason nobody wanted to transfer in was that Howard ran his department with the quiet gravity of a man who understood, in his bones, that work was serious. Problems were serious. Deadlines were serious. Performance reviews were serious. Howard was not humorless exactly, but the laughter was calibrated, deployed at the correct intervals, and did not linger past the moment that generated it.

His team produced good work. They also, every single one of them, applied for transfers with a frequency that Howard had never quite connected to his management style, because his management style felt to Howard like the obvious and correct response to a professional environment, which was to take it seriously.

Down the hall, in the department that handled the same function for a different region, worked a manager named Patricia Osei. Patricia's team had a waiting list.

The differences between the two departments were not differences of workload or compensation or the quality of the coffee, which came from the same machine in the same break room. They were differences of atmosphere. Howard's department felt like a library in which something important was always at stake. Patricia's department felt like a place where people were genuinely glad to be.

Patricia had instituted, years earlier and with no particular theoretical framework behind it, what she called the Two-Minute Rule. The Two-Minute Rule held that at any point during the workday, any member of the team could invoke two minutes of complete departure from whatever was happening. Two minutes to show the group something funny, tell a story that had nothing to do with work, or ask a question that was entirely irrelevant to the quarterly targets, such as: what is the correct way to eat a

Reese's Peanut Butter Cup? Or: if you had to describe this spreadsheet as a weather pattern, what would it be?

The questions were not the point. The laughter was the point. And what Patricia had observed, over years of managing people through genuinely difficult periods, was that the team that could still laugh on Friday afternoon at three o'clock, after a week that had genuinely tested them, was a team that would be fine on Monday morning.

Howard became aware of the atmospheric difference the way most managers become aware of things they have been not-quite-seeing for a long time: through a conversation he did not expect to have.

It was a Tuesday afternoon in March, and one of his best analysts, a young woman named Simone, came to his office and told him she was applying for a transfer. Howard asked, as he always asked in these conversations, whether there was anything he could have done differently.

Simone said: "Howard, I like you and I think you're a good manager. I just need to work somewhere where people laugh more."

Howard sat with this for a moment. "We laugh," he said.

"When something is funny," Simone said, carefully. "But we don't make room for it. It just sort of happens by accident sometimes, and then everyone goes back to the serious thing."

Turning Point

Halfway through the next Monday meeting, Howard stopped. His team looked at him.

"Can I ask you something completely unrelated to any of this?" he said. "If this department were a type of weather, what would it be?"

There was a silence of approximately four seconds, and then someone said: "A weather advisory." Someone else said: "Overcast with a chance of more overcast." Someone else said: "One of those days where it's not raining but you can tell it wants to."

Howard laughed. Not the calibrated laugh from the holiday party. An actual laugh, the kind that arrives before you decide to produce it. His team laughed with him. Not politely. Actually.

He started his Monday meetings with what he called the question of the week, always irrelevant to the work and always genuinely curious. The questions took four minutes. His team began arriving before the meetings were scheduled to start, which had not previously happened.

Simone withdrew her transfer request four months later. She did not make a production of this. She simply stopped pursuing it in the way that people stop pursuing exits when the reason they wanted to leave has been addressed.

Howard noticed. He did not mention it to her. He simply kept going. The question of the week. The permission to laugh. The two minutes. The metrics, which Howard watched carefully because he was still Howard and some things do not change, did not suffer. If anything, they improved slightly in the following two quarters.

What he could say, and did say when asked, was that his team seemed happier. And that happy teams, in his experience, produced better work. And that the investment required had been approximately four minutes per Monday morning, and the willingness to answer the weather question honestly.

Which, for the record, he had eventually answered himself. His department, he said, used to be a weather advisory. It was working on becoming partly sunny with a good chance of clearing.

The team applauded with a sincerity he had not expected and that, he admitted afterward, had genuinely moved him. Simone had started the applause.

Lesson

Howard had run a serious department for twelve years and produced good results. He started running a department where people laughed on purpose and produced better ones. The difference was four minutes on Monday mornings and the willingness to answer a question about weather.

What Patricia had understood, and what Howard eventually learned, is that laughter is not the opposite of seriousness. It is the pressure release that makes sustained seriousness possible. A team that never laughs is a team operating at maximum pressure all the time, and maximum pressure, maintained without relief, does not produce maximum performance. It produces the quiet, building tension that eventually sends the best people down the hall to the department with the waiting list.

The physics are not complicated. It is genuinely hard to sustain worry, anxiety, and the particular weight of accumulated professional pressure when you are laughing. The laughter interrupts the accumulation. It does not solve the problem on the whiteboard or close the gap in the quarterly numbers. But it returns the people working on those things to a state in which they are capable of their best thinking, which turns out to be the prerequisite for everything else.

Some of the most important management decisions are the smallest ones. A question about weather. Permission to laugh. Two minutes. This was one of them.

The Incredible Shrinking Belt

Situation

There is a saying among submariners that life at sea consists of many hours of boredom followed by moments of sheer terror. This is not entirely accurate. What fills the hours is the particular creativity of a group of people with sharp minds, limited space, and a collective interest in finding something to laugh about.

Submariners are, as a category, among the most inventive human beings I have ever encountered. Put a group of them in a sealed metal tube for weeks at a time with no sunlight and no outside world, and they will develop an interior culture of humor so refined that outsiders cannot fully appreciate it. The laughter is not incidental to submarine life. It is load bearing.

The other thing worth knowing is the food. The food on a United States submarine is genuinely extraordinary. Great dinners. Remarkable breakfasts. Sticky buns on weekend mornings that constituted, in the vocabulary of submarine culture, a form of institutional love. The predictable consequence is that submariners gain weight at sea. Most handle this with the resigned good humor of people who understand the bargain they have made. Extraordinary sticky buns. Slightly tighter uniform. Fair trade.

Then there was Lieutenant Whitfield.

He was a new officer, technically capable, and possessed of a quality that experienced submariners recognize and quietly file away: he treated the enlisted men with a subtle condescension that he probably did not register in himself and that they registered immediately. He was also weight-conscious in the particular way of a vain person, not for health reasons but because his appearance mattered to him in a way that his relationship with his crew did not.

He announced his weight concerns regularly. The enlisted crew watched him for several weeks and made their assessment. Then they made their plan.

The poopy suit is the working uniform of the submariner: a Navy-blue jumpsuit cinched with a web belt with a brass buckle. The web belt is adjustable in a simple and irreversible way: you cut off the excess. It fits perfectly, which also means that if someone were to trim a small amount from the end, the belt would fit slightly more snugly without the difference being immediately detectable.

I do not know who originated the plan. The authorship was collective, distributed across the enlisted crew with the democratic efficiency that submarine culture produces when it is motivated. Every few days, when Lieutenant Whitfield's belt was accessible, a small portion disappeared. Not enough to notice in a single observation. Enough to accumulate.

The genius of the prank was its timeline. A prank that produces immediate results is a joke. A prank that unfolds over weeks, requiring patience and coordination and the collective discipline of multiple people maintaining a secret, is something closer to performance art.

Lieutenant Whitfield began noticing that his belt was feeling tighter. He mentioned this. He mentioned it more than once. The enlisted men received these announcements with expressions of sympathetic concern that were, under the circumstances, acts of considerable professional restraint. He concluded that he was gaining weight. He was not gaining weight. The belt was losing length.

His response was entirely consistent with his character: he became more vocal about his expanding waistline and more ostentatious about his attempts to address it. He started declining portions at meals and announcing his sacrifice. The sticky buns, which he had previously eaten with everyone else, were declined with visible effort. The belt continued to shrink.

Turning Point

The prank unraveled the way slow pranks eventually unravel: the consequences outpaced the comedy. Lieutenant Whitfield stopped eating in a way that crossed from theatrical into genuinely concerning. He was losing weight. Nobody wanted to be responsible for an officer's health. Nobody wanted to explain to the commanding officer that a member of the wardroom was medically declining because the enlisted crew had been gradually removing portions of his belt.

The prank was revealed.

Lieutenant Whitfield, to his credit, made a choice in the days following the revelation. He could have responded with the formal authority available to an officer whose enlisted crew had pranked him for weeks. He did not take it. He came to the mess the following morning, picked up a sticky bun, and said to the table at large: "I checked my belt this morning. It appears to be the correct length."

The table laughed. Not carefully. Actually. He laughed with them. That laugh cost him something and produced something, and the something it produced was the beginning of a different relationship with the crew that served under him. He was never again the officer he had been before the belt. He was, by most assessments, a better one.

Lesson

The belt story carries two lessons that arrive in the same package.

The first is about humor: the laughter is not the opposite of the work. It is the thing that makes the work sustainable. A crew that can construct a multi-week operation requiring patience, coordination, and collective restraint is a crew that is fully engaged with each other, and a crew that is fully engaged with each other is exactly the crew you want when the hours of boredom give way to the moments of something else.

The second is about leadership. Lieutenant Whitfield's crew did not prank him because they were bored. They pranked him because he had given them a target. His vanity, his condescension, his public self-concern in an environment that rewards collective humility: these created the conditions for what followed. His recovery, the sticky bun, and the laugh, were his actual leadership debut on that submarine. Everything before it had been performance. That moment was genuine, and the crew recognized the difference immediately, because crews always do.

Treat your people well. And when you suspect something is going wrong, check your belt before you blame your stomach. The problem is not always where you think it is.

Chapter 16

SERVICE / HELPING OTHERS HELPS US

One of the quietest and most reliable sources of happiness is also one of the least advertised: being useful to someone other than yourself.

The culture does not market this aggressively because usefulness does not look glamorous from a distance. It rarely photographs well. It does not lend itself to the language of status. Service is usually local, practical, and often invisible. A meal delivered. A call returned. A younger colleague encouraged. A frightened person accompanied. A struggling business owner coached through a difficult season. A neighbor's trash cans brought in without being asked. None of this is dramatic. Nearly all of it matters.

I have spent enough time in leadership, coaching, and military service to notice a pattern. The people who seem most fundamentally alive are not always the ones with the most freedom, money, or recognition. They are often the ones who have found a way to direct their energy outward. Their lives are not free of difficulty. But difficulty does not consume all available oxygen because purpose is moving through the room.

Helping others helps us partly because it interrupts one of the mind's worst habits: endless self-reference. Left to itself, the mind becomes a closed loop. How am I doing? How do I look? What am I missing? Why did that happen to me? Am I behind?

The loop is exhausting. Service breaks it open. Someone else enters the frame, and with them comes proportion.

The Relief of Being Useful

Situation

I once watched a man move through retirement with increasing restlessness. His career had been substantial and successful. He held authority, made decisions, and carried responsibility that affected many people. Then he retired, and the world, quite reasonably, stopped asking him to do those particular things. He was healthy, financially secure, and by every conventional measure fortunate. He was also, within a year, noticeably diminished.

What he missed was not merely the schedule. It was usefulness.

Turning Point

He eventually began volunteering one morning a week with a local organization that provided mentoring and practical support for young adults entering the workforce. He helped with résumés, mock interviews, workplace habits, and the thousand small forms of translation that are obvious to someone who has spent decades in organizations and bewildering to someone just entering them.

The change in him was disproportionate to the number of hours involved. One morning a week should not have been enough to alter a person's entire posture toward life. And yet it was. His voice had more energy in it. His stories regained color. His weeks had a shape again. He had moved from being occupied to being needed, and those are not remotely the same thing.

Need is not always pleasant. In fact, it can be burdensome. But meaningful need, chosen freely and carried in proportion, is one of the great animating forces in a happy life.

Service and Happiness

There is a misunderstanding worth correcting here. Service is not the same thing as self-erasure. Some people hear a chapter like this and imagine burnout disguised as virtue: the person who says yes to everything, neglects their own health, and confuses exhaustion with nobility. That is not what I mean.

The service that nourishes happiness is service offered from health, not service extracted through guilt. It is the kind that connects a person to meaning rather than depleting them into resentment. The difference matters. Helping others at the expense of your own integrity, sleep, marriage, or sanity is not virtue. It is bad management with a halo.

Healthy service has boundaries. It also has joy.

In every chapter of life, there are forms of service available that fit the season. A young parent serves by staying present to children who did not ask to be born and now need everything. A professional serves by using competence to make an organization healthier rather than merely using the organization as a ladder. An older adult serves by becoming the kind of elder whose steadiness lowers the temperature in every room they enter.

The form changes. The principle does not. When life is organized only around personal comfort, it starts to feel strangely small. When it includes contribution, it expands.

The Unexpected Return

One of the most surprising things about helping others is how often the help returns through a different door than the one it left through. Not always materially. Often emotionally. The person who mentors discovers that they are being reminded why their own work matters. The person who visits someone in the hospital drives home with a sharper appreciation for their own ordinary health. The person who volunteers once a month finds friendships forming in the very place they thought they were going merely to contribute.

This is not why we should serve. Service offered only for the emotional return is a disguised transaction. But the return is real nonetheless, and it is one of the reasons service belongs in any honest conversation about happiness.

The happiest people I know are almost never sealed off. They are permeable. Their lives have openings through which care moves outward.

Fun First, Business Second

There is a particular kind of professional challenge that I have always been drawn to, and I want to be honest about that at the outset, because it matters to how this story is understood.

I like failing organizations.

Not because I enjoy other people's difficulties, but because a failing organization is one of the few professional environments where the work is completely unambiguous. Nobody is arguing about priorities when the building is on fire. Nobody is protecting territory when the territory is already lost. The path forward may be unclear, but the need to find one is not. I have always done my best work in those conditions, and when an opportunity came to take over one of the worst-performing operations in our company, I did not hesitate.

I should have asked more questions.

Situation

The conversation that preceded my arrival described a struggling operation with declining numbers and some leadership challenges that had created personnel issues. The framing was honest as far as it went. What it did not convey with any precision was the rate at which the salespeople were leaving, which meant the numbers I had been given for the size of the operation were not the numbers I would find when I arrived. People were walking out the door during the recruitment process, and by the time I got there, the gap between the described operation and the actual one was significant.

Two managers had been running separate geographical areas. Those areas were combined under my leadership, which was presented as a streamlining. What it actually meant was that two cultures of unhappiness, each with its own inventory of grievances and its own history of poor management, were now sharing one roof. The previous managers had, over time, produced a level of negativity in those offices that I had not seen in a long time. People were not just unhappy. They were committed to their unhappiness in the way that people become committed to it when they have been carrying it long enough that it starts to feel like an accurate assessment of reality rather than a reaction to specific circumstances.

And they kept leaving. Not in a rush, but steadily, in the way that an organization bleeds out when the underlying wound is not addressed. Each departure made the math worse, because costs were shared and the remaining people carried more of them, and the financial pressure intensified the negativity, and the negativity produced more departures. The spiral had its own momentum. I was not stopping it. I was arriving into it.

The expenses kept rising. The headcount kept shrinking. I ran the numbers in several different directions and kept arriving at the same uncomfortable conclusion: we might need to shut down the current operation entirely, find a way out from under the existing obligations, and rebuild somewhere else with people who had not been marinating in years of bad leadership.

And then we reached the moment I still think about.

One more departure would trigger the shutdown. There was one person, one individual, whose decision about whether to stay or go would determine whether the operation survived. That is not a position any leader wants to be in. It is also, I have come to understand, exactly the position that clarifies what you actually believe and what you are actually made of.

That person decided to stay. Not because the numbers were good, because they were not. Not because the future was clear, because it was not. They decided to stay to see whether I could do what I had said I could do. They gave me a chance based on nothing more than a judgment about whether I was the kind of person who kept their word.

I have never forgotten that.

Turning Point

I called everyone together.

I want to describe what that room looked like, because it matters. These were people who had been through years of poor leadership, who had watched colleagues leave, who were sharing costs that kept rising, who had been managing their own disappointment for long enough that their faces had settled into a kind of guarded neutrality. They were not hostile. They were waiting. They had heard things before.

I told them the truth, which was that the operation was in serious trouble, that I was not going to pretend otherwise, and that

I did not know for certain that we would turn it around. Those things were true and they deserved to hear them.

Then I told them something that surprised them.

I told them that one of the problems with our performance was the attitude in the office. Not any individual person's attitude, not a quality I was attributing to bad character or weak commitment. The collective attitude. The atmosphere. The experience of walking through the door every morning into a place that felt like a problem rather than a possibility. That atmosphere was affecting everything, and it was not going to change on its own, and changing it was not the responsibility of leadership alone. It was everyone's responsibility. Mine first, but not mine exclusively. And then I told them the motto we were going to operate by going forward.

Fun first. Business second.

I want to be precise about what I meant, because it was not a slogan designed to make people feel better about a bad situation. It was a statement about sequence and about cause. The business results we needed were not going to be produced by a group of people who dreaded coming to work. They were going to be produced, if they were going to be produced at all, by a group of people who had some genuine reason to be there beyond obligation. The fun was not the reward for turning the operation around. The fun was the condition for it.

I also told them something about complaining, because complaining was woven into the culture in a way that was actively corrosive. I told them I was not opposed to complaints. I had complaints of my own. Complaints, properly directed, are useful information. What I would not accept was complaints circulating through the office freely, landing on people who had no ability to address them and no reason to carry them, bringing down the general atmosphere one conversation at a time.

If you need to complain, I said, come to my office. Close the door. Tell me everything. I am listening and I will take it seriously. But what happens in this office when the door is open is not a vehicle for grievances. It is a place where we are building something, and we are going to protect that.

What changed first was the atmosphere. Not dramatically, not all at once, but gradually and then more quickly, the way that cultural shifts actually happen. Someone laughed in the office at something genuinely funny and nobody looked around to check whether that was appropriate. A small win got celebrated instead of minimized. A complaint went to my office with the door closed and came back out without circulating. Another departure did not happen. And then another.

The person who had stayed to see whether I could keep my word watched all of this and made a decision, quietly and without announcing it, to become an asset rather than a question mark. The others made similar decisions on similar timelines.

And then the numbers began to move.

Lesson

We turned the operation around. Not quickly, and not without cost, and not in the way that I would have designed if I had known at the outset what I was actually walking into. But we turned it around, and we became one of the top producing organizations in the company, which is a sentence I do not say without thinking about the person who stayed when they could have left and what that decision made possible.

The lesson I carry is about the sequence.

The conventional assumption in struggling organizations is that performance must improve before attitudes can improve, that the results will change the culture once they arrive. I believe the opposite is true. Culture changes first, or performance does not change at all. The attitudes in that office were not a symptom of the poor results, though the poor results had made them worse. They were a cause. Addressing the cause was the prerequisite for everything else.

Fun first. Business second.

Not because fun is more important than business. Because in a damaged organization, with damaged people carrying years of damaged culture, the business cannot come first. It cannot come first because the people who are supposed to produce it are not in a condition to produce it. You have to address the condition. You have to give them a reason to be there, a genuine one, before they will give the operation what the operation needs.

And if you do it right, if you are consistent and patient and willing to absorb the skepticism of people who have been disappointed before, the business catches up. It always catches up. People who are genuinely glad to come to work produce better results than people who are not. This is not a motivational observation. It is an operational one.

I learned it in an office that was one more resignation away from being shut down, from a group of people who decided, slowly and without fanfare, to build something worth coming to.

Where This Becomes Practical

If you are reading this chapter and wondering what form this takes in your own life, begin with the most ordinary question available: who around me could be helped by something I already know how to do?

The answer is usually close at hand. A younger colleague who needs coaching. A church class that needs teaching. A nonprofit that needs board members who actually read financial statements. A neighbor who needs a ride. A family member who needs less advice and more presence. A grandchild who needs a listening adult. A veteran trying to navigate civilian life. A student who does not yet know what professional world they belong to.

Service becomes daunting only when we imagine it must be large. Most of the service that changes lives is small and repeated.

A final word: helping others does not guarantee happiness, but a life devoid of contribution almost guarantees a thinner version of it. We are built, it seems to me, not only to receive love and meaning but to transmit them. A life that does both is far more durable than a life organized around acquisition alone.

People often ask what the purpose of the later chapters of life is once the career has shifted, the children have grown, and the old structures no longer demand what they used to demand. One answer, not the only one but a very good one, is this: to become useful in ways younger people cannot yet imagine.

That is not a consolation prize. It is one of the great privileges of age.

Part IV

HAPPINESS LATER IN LIFE

What the later chapters teach us that the earlier ones couldn't

Opening Reflection: Watching the Next Generation Rise

Two stories illuminate that truth especially well. The first is about watching a child find his own path. The second is about watching a grandfather become most beloved after life removed the very qualities that had once made him formidable.

There is a particular happiness that belongs to the later chapters of a life that is not fully available in the earlier ones: the happiness of watching someone you love become themselves. Not the version of themselves you imagined when they were young, and the future felt like something you could still shape. The actual version, the one they arrived at through their own choices and their own struggles and their own slow discovery of what they were built for.

This happiness requires something that does not come naturally to most parents: the willingness to release the blueprint. The blueprint is drawn from love, but it is also drawn from the parents' own map of what a successful life looks like. Children, almost without exception, have a different map. The tension between those two maps is one of the defining experiences of parenthood, and the resolution of it, when it comes, is one of the most profound satisfactions available to a human being.

Every parent carries a quiet blueprint for how their child's story is supposed to go. Good grades, steady progress, the right milestones arriving on schedule. It is not a selfish blueprint. It comes from love, and from wanting to spare them the harder roads.

But children have a way of folding that blueprint in half and handing it back to you. And the parents who learn to let go of the blueprint, to trust what they cannot see yet, are usually the ones who get to watch something extraordinary happen.

The hardest part of parenting well, in my experience, is the sustained discipline of distinguishing between helping and intervening. Helping keeps the door open and the encouragement flowing while the child does the actual work of becoming themselves. Intervening substitutes the parent's judgment for the child's development. The two feel similar in the moment. They produce very different results over time.

Watching Children Succeed

Every child is a mystery that unfolds on its own schedule. The mistake most parents make, and I made it too, is assuming that the schedule should match the one we arrived at parenthood carrying. Our son had a different schedule, a different set of native strengths, and a different path to his own version of success. The job was to stay present while he found it. That turned out to be harder and more rewarding than anything we could have designed for him.

Situation

Our son was bright, genuinely, unmistakably bright. Anyone who spent time with him could see it. But school measures intelligence in a fairly narrow way, and his particular kind didn't always cooperate with that system. Reading came hard. Sitting still and absorbing came hard. Doing, building, figuring out, getting his hands on something, and working through it came naturally and with a focus that was almost startling to watch.

He was a doer in a world that kept asking him to be a reader.

As a parent, you want to help. Sometimes help looks like stepping in. And stepping in, if you are not careful, can quietly communicate to a child that you don't fully trust them to find their own way. We had to learn, more than once, to step back.

Turning Point

What he found, on his own terms and in his own time, was Information Technology. Not as a subject to study but as a world to inhabit. He learned by doing what he had always done best, and the fluency he developed went well beyond what any classroom had offered him.

Watching that happen was one of those parenting moments that quietly corrects your assumptions. The blueprint we had been holding turned out to be unnecessary. He had his own.

And when it came to the most personal chapter of all, he was patient there too. He did not settle. He waited for the right person rather than simply the available one.

Lesson

He went on to become Chief Operating Officer for a medical technology company and an authority in the emerging IT landscape, a man whose career is built on exactly the kind of hands-on mastery that his early years quietly promised, if you knew how to read the signals. He married the love of his life. Not early. At the right time.

Our job was never to clear every obstacle from the path. It was to stay present, stay encouraging, and trust that the person we were raising had something inside him that we could support but could not install.

He didn't need a different path. He needed permission to take his own.

The COO title and the marriage to the right person are the visible outcomes. What is less visible, and more important, is the journey that produced them: the years of working through difficulty without the conventional markers of progress, the patience that built in him qualities that the fast track might never have required, the deep fluency in a field he genuinely loved because he came to it through curiosity rather than compliance. The blueprint we were holding would have produced a different person. The person who emerged from his own path is more capable and more himself than anything our blueprint would have built.

Watching children succeed is one of the deepest happinesses available to a parent. What makes it deepest is when the success belongs entirely to them, when you can look at what they have built and know with certainty that it is theirs, that you contributed to the conditions and the encouragement and the long, patient act of staying present, and they contributed everything else. That particular happiness is not available to the parent who cleared every obstacle. It belongs to the one who learned to step back and watch.

The Grandparent Revelation

Every culture that has ever existed has understood something that modern professional life tends to obscure: the elderly have something the achiever does not. Not competence, not ambition, not the focused drive that gets things built and organizations run, and careers advanced. Something quieter and harder to name. The capacity to be fully present with another person. The patience to listen without already formulating the response. The wisdom to know that the grandchild climbing into your lap is not an interruption of something more important. It is the most important thing.

My father did not arrive at this capacity through intention. He arrived at it through a medical crisis that removed everything else and left him with what was underneath. What was underneath turned out to be more than anyone, including him, had known was there. This chapter is about what I learned watching it emerge, and what it suggested to me about the version of myself I was still in the process of becoming.

We spend the first half of our lives acquiring the qualities we admire in our role models, and sometimes the second half discovering that the qualities we needed most were not the ones we spent the first half chasing. My father taught me this in the most unexpected way imaginable, and I was too busy grieving the version of him I had lost to notice what the new version was teaching me, until I finally stopped looking backward long enough to see what was directly in front of me.

Situation

My father was the standard I measured everything against.

Straight A student. Competitive athlete. A businessman who rose rapidly to president of not one but two companies. The relatives had a phrase they used about me, repeated often enough that it became a kind of identity: you are just like your father. His competitive spirit was my competitive spirit. His drive was my inheritance.

Then came the knee surgery. He had been selected for a dream promotion, the kind of opportunity that arrives once in a career and redefines everything that follows. Before he could step into it, the knee had to be addressed. A routine procedure. He went in for surgery and never quite came back the same.

Something went seriously wrong that night. They found him near death, in a coma. The doctors saved his life, but he remained in that coma for three days. The rehabilitation was long and grinding, five months at a major rehab facility.

When he came home, the man who returned was not the man who left. The competitive fire was gone. The laser focus on business, on performance, on winning, gone. My role model had not died, but the version of him I had patterned myself after had. And I grieved that, privately and longer than I admitted to anyone.

Turning Point

He began spending time with the younger siblings. With the grandchildren. Not structured time, not coaching or instructing, just time. He told them stories. He asked about their lives and actually listened to the answers. He encouraged them in the unhurried way of a man who was no longer racing toward anything.

I watched the grandchildren respond to him and saw something I had not anticipated: they revered him. Not out of obligation or respect for a title. Out of genuine, uncomplicated love for a man who made them feel seen.

The warmth that had replaced his competitive edge was not a diminishment. It was a different kind of strength; one I had never thought to develop because I had been so busy becoming the version of him I already understood.

Lesson

My father taught me twice. The first time through his ambition and his refusal to finish second. The second time, after the surgery and the coma and the long road back, he taught me something the first version of him never could have: that presence is its own form of leadership. That warmth is not the consolation prize for people who couldn't manage success.

I had spent years believing that the father who returned from that hospital was a diminished version of the one I lost. What I eventually understood was that he had become something more complete: a man whose full range had finally been allowed to surface, not because he chose it, but because life removed everything else and left him with what mattered most.

The people who remember us most clearly, and love us most durably, are rarely the ones who watched us win. They are the ones we slowed down for.

There is something worth sitting with in the specifics of what changed for my father after the surgery, and the coma, and the long rehabilitation. He did not choose to become warmer, or more present, or more interested in the people around him. Life removed the things that had been consuming his attention, the career ambitions, the competitive drive, the perpetual forward momentum toward the next achievement, and what remained, once those things were gone, was the person underneath them. That person, it turned out, was extraordinary in ways that the driven, successful, competitive version had never had room to be.

I do not recommend a coma as the path to this discovery. But I do think the discovery itself is available without one, to anyone willing to ask, honestly, what would remain if the career and the titles and the achievements were taken away tomorrow. What is there, underneath the accomplishments? Who are you when you are not performing? The grandchildren climbing into my father's lap were not receiving a diminished version of him. They were receiving the complete version, the one that had always been there and had finally been given space to show itself.

Chapter 17
THE EMPTY NEST SURPRISE

The empty nest is often described as a loss, and of course, it is one. The house becomes quiet. The routines disappear. The role that gave structure to decades of life suddenly changes shape. But if that were the whole story, this chapter would be a lament. It is not. It is a chapter about rediscovery.

The transition to an empty nest is discussed almost entirely in terms of loss: the quiet house, the absent children, the role that has been so central to a parent's identity for so long, suddenly rendered optional. What gets less attention, because it is harder to see until you are inside it, is the rediscovery that waits on the other side of that loss. Carol and Michael did not plan to find each other again. They had never lost each other exactly. They had simply been so thoroughly organized around their children that they had stopped organizing anything around themselves.

Situation

For twenty-three years, Carol and Michael had organized their lives around the needs of other people. Three children in eleven years meant the house had never been quiet, the calendar had never been empty, and the two of them had never really been alone.

Their youngest left for college on a Saturday in August. They drove her to campus, carried boxes up three flights of stairs, hugged her goodbye in a parking lot while trying to look like people who were fine. They drove home largely in silence. Carol cried somewhere around the second hour. Michael handed her the napkins from the glove compartment because he had learned, over twenty-three years, to keep napkins in the glove compartment.

They walked into a house that was immaculate and absolutely silent.

For the first several months, they filled the silence with logistics. They were busy in the way that people are busy when they are not quite ready to sit with something. What they were not ready to sit with was each other. Not because anything was wrong. But because they had spent two decades as co-managers of a very demanding operation and had quietly stopped being something else to one another.

Turning Point

In February, seven months after their youngest left, Michael made a reservation. Not for a special occasion. Just a Tuesday night at a restaurant they had talked about trying for two years. He told Carol to be ready at seven.

They sat at that restaurant for three hours. They talked about things they hadn't discussed in years and things they had never discussed at all. Michael ordered dessert, which he never did. Carol told a story she had forgotten to mention, and they found it hilarious, and then sat for a moment in the comfortable quiet of two people who have known each other for a long time.

Driving home, Carol said, "We should do this every week."

They did.

Lesson

Carol and Michael had not lost each other during the parenting years. They had simply set each other down in a safe place and trusted, without discussing it, that the other would still be there when the house got quiet. They were right. But trust is not the same as attention. And attention, once they started paying it again, turned out to be the simplest and most renewable gift they had to offer one another.

The person you chose, before all of it, before the school plays and the orthodontist appointments and the college parking lots, is still there. A little older. Recognizable in all the ways that matter. Tuesday nights at a restaurant turned out to be a good place to start.

The napkins in the glove compartment are the detail I keep returning to. Michael had learned, over twenty-three years, to keep napkins in the glove compartment. Not because Carol cried often, but because he had been paying that kind of attention to her for long enough that the knowledge had become automatic, built into the way he maintained the car, the way other habits are built into the way we maintain ourselves. That is what twenty-three years of genuine partnership produces. The question the empty nest asked them was whether they still had access to each other underneath all the logistics, and the answer turned out to be yes, absolutely yes, available on any Tuesday evening they cared to test it.

If there is a practical suggestion embedded in this story, it is simply this: do not wait for the house to empty before you make the reservation. The restaurant has been there for two years. The person across the table from you has been there longer. Tuesday nights are available now.

What Thirty-One Years Actually Looks Like

Catherine and David were not, by the standards of the stories people tell about marriage, a romantic couple.

They did not finish each other's sentences. They did not gaze at each other across rooms at parties. They disagreed fairly regularly about money, about how often to visit David's mother, and about whether the thermostat should be set at sixty-eight or seventy-one, a disagreement that had been ongoing for thirty-one years and showed no signs of resolution. David thought Catherine drove too fast. Catherine thought David drove too slowly. They had taken separate cars on road trips twice.

They were also, by any honest assessment, deeply and durably happy together. This confused people who expected marriage to look like something else, and it confused Catherine and David not at all, because they had stopped expecting it to look like anything in particular sometime around year seven and had simply started paying attention to what it actually was.

What it actually was, was this.

David made coffee every morning. He had made the coffee every morning for thirty-one years, without being asked, without requiring acknowledgment, without any of the careful ledger-keeping that some couples bring to the distribution of household labor. He made it before Catherine was awake, set her cup on the left side of the counter where she would see it immediately, and left for his run. She drank it alone in the kitchen for twenty minutes before the day began. She had told him once, early in the marriage, that those twenty minutes were among her favorites of the day. He had never forgotten. He had never stopped.

Catherine remembered things. Not the important things, the birthdays and the anniversaries, which both of them managed adequately. The small things. That David's back was worse on Wednesdays after the commute. That the particular silence he produced at the dinner table on certain evenings meant he had

had the kind of day that needed to be let alone rather than probed. That he had been carrying a conversation with his brother unresolved for three months and needed to be gently redirected toward finishing it before it became something heavier. She paid attention to him in the specific, granular way that accumulates over decades into something that looks, from the outside, like intuition.

It was not intuition. It was thirty-one years of paying attention.

They had been through the things that most marriages of thirty-one years go through, which is to say they had been through a great deal.

A miscarriage before their first child, which had put a particular weight on the marriage for two years that they had navigated less gracefully than either of them would have preferred, and which they had eventually navigated through rather than around, which turned out to matter.

A period in year fourteen when David's company restructured and his professional identity, which had been more load-bearing than he had known, went through a reckoning that was slow and uncomfortable and required Catherine to be patient in ways she did not always feel patient. She had been patient anyway. She had not been perfect about it. She had been consistent.

Catherine's mother's illness, which had lasted four years and required a kind of sustained, unglamorous caregiving that fell primarily to Catherine simply because of geography, and which David had supported not through grand gestures but through the daily, unremarkable accumulation of covering what needed to be covered so she could cover what only she could cover.

Neither of them would describe these as the best years of their marriage. But both of them would say, if pressed, that those years were when they learned what the marriage actually was. Not the version of it that had been visible at the wedding, which was optimistic and lovely and real as far as it went. The version underneath, which was built from smaller and less photogenic materials: patience, consistency, the willingness to absorb the weight of a difficult season without keeping score, and the decision, made repeatedly and without ceremony, to stay in the room.

They went to dinner on their thirty-first anniversary at the same restaurant where they had gone on their first date, which was a thing they did every year and which their children found either deeply romantic or mildly embarrassing, depending on the year.

Over dinner, their younger daughter, who was home from college and had offered to drive them so they could both have a glass of wine, asked them the question that children of long marriages eventually ask:

What is the secret?

Catherine and David looked at each other.

"There isn't one," Catherine said.

"There's a practice," David said. "Which is different."

Their daughter waited.

"You keep paying attention," Catherine said. "That's mostly it. You keep paying attention to the actual person, not the person you've decided they are, not the person you remember from ten years ago. The one who's sitting across from you right now. They change. You change. If you stop paying attention, you end up in a marriage with someone you think you know but don't anymore. Which is a lonelier place than being single."

"What he does," David said, "is make the coffee. What she does is remember what the silence means." He paused. "That's probably not very useful as advice."

"It's the most useful thing anyone has ever told me about marriage," their daughter said.

She meant it. She has thought about it many times since.

The thing that the story of Catherine and David's marriage offers, which the romantic version of long marriages rarely does, is an accurate picture of what durability actually requires. Not the grand gestures, not the passionate declarations, not the version that looks good in the retelling. The coffee made before anyone is awake. The silence read correctly. The patience maintained imperfectly but consistently through the difficult years. The decision, unremarkable and renewable, to keep paying attention to the person who is actually there.

Thirty-one years of that is not a love story in the conventional sense. It is something more useful: evidence that the conventional sense is not the only one, and not the most durable one, and not the one that produces the kind of happiness that still looks like itself at a restaurant table on a thirty-first anniversary, with a daughter who asked the right question and listened carefully to the answer.

Lesson

Catherine and David did not set out to build an extraordinary marriage. They set out to build a life together, and the marriage was what happened when two people kept paying attention to each other through the full range of what a life actually contains.

Thirty-one years is not a number. It is an accumulation. It is the coffee every morning and the thermostat disagreement and the miscarriage and the restructuring and the mother's illness and the Tuesday nights and the ten thousand ordinary moments that do not photograph well and do not get posted anywhere and do not look, from the outside, like anything worth noting. From the inside, they are everything.

What Catherine and David understood, without ever making a speech about it, is that a long marriage is not maintained by the grand gestures. It is maintained by the small consistent ones. The attention that does not require a special occasion. The presence that shows up on a Wednesday because Wednesday is when it is needed, not because Wednesday is particularly convenient. The willingness, accumulated over decades, to keep paying attention to the actual person rather than the idea of the person you married.

The research on long marriages is consistent on this point: the couples who stay together and remain genuinely happy are not the ones who never conflict. They are the ones who have developed, over time, a reliable way of returning to each other after conflict. Not the ones who never drift. The ones who notice the drift and close the distance. Not the ones who always feel the warmth. The ones who tend the warmth on the mornings when it is not obvious.

The coffee is not a small thing. It is the whole thing, made visible in a cup.

Chapter 18

SIMPLE JOY

Simple joy has a poor publicist. It is modest, repeatable, and usually located in ordinary places. Because of that, ambitious people often miss it while looking for larger proof that life is going well. The stories in this chapter are about people who discovered, in different ways, that a quiet life can still be a rich one.

Contentment is one of those qualities that is easy to mistake for its lesser cousins: passivity, low ambition, and a failure of imagination. The person who is genuinely content with what they have is sometimes assumed to have simply not wanted more, as though contentment were the default state of the unambitious rather than the earned condition of someone who has done the harder work of knowing what they actually value.

Millard was not without ambition. He was without confusion about what his ambitions were for.

Situation

Nobody who drove through Millard's part of town would have slowed down to take a second look.

The house was small, a two-bedroom frame structure he had inherited from his parents and maintained with the kind of stubborn, unhurried care that has nothing to do with impressing anyone and everything to do with respect. The truck in the driveway was fourteen years old and started every morning, which was the only standard Millard held it to.

He worked at the same manufacturing plant for thirty-one years. He coached youth baseball for sixteen years, long past the age when his own children had moved through the program, staying because the kids kept coming and he kept enjoying it. He had dinner with his wife, Eleanor, most nights of their marriage at the same kitchen table, and they talked the way people talk when they have not outsourced their evenings to distraction and obligation.

His neighbors knew him by name. His neighbors' children knew him by name. The man at the hardware store had his coffee ready before Millard reached the counter on Saturday mornings. These were not small things to Millard. These were the architecture of everything.

Millard had not chosen simplicity as a statement. He had simply, from a young age, known what he valued and organized his days around it without apology and without comparison. He had never once, as far as anyone could tell, spent significant energy wanting to be somewhere other than where he was.

That is rarer than it sounds. And it is, it turns out, the heart of the whole thing.

Turning Point

Contentment is not the consolation prize for people who didn't want enough. It is the achievement of people who wanted the right things clearly enough that they recognized them when they had them.

What Millard understood, and what I have come to believe after watching a great many people build their lives around impressive materials that left them strangely hollow, is that the architecture of a happy life is not built from impressive materials. It is built from specific ones. The specific person who is glad to see you. The specific work that makes an afternoon disappear. The specific Saturday morning ritual that requires nothing more than coffee and a familiar face behind a counter who already knows your order.

Specificity is the whole thing. Not the generic good life, but the specific one. The one built from things that are genuinely yours, not borrowed from someone else's idea of what a life should look like. Millard had been building that specific life, without apology or explanation or any particular awareness that it was remarkable, since the day he inherited a two-bedroom house and decided it was enough. It was not that he had low standards. It was that his standards were his own.

Lesson

Millard is not a cautionary tale about ambition. He is not an argument for small lives or modest expectations. He is something more specific and more useful: a demonstration that contentment is not what happens when you fail to want more. It is what happens when you decide, clearly and without apology, what actually matters to you and build accordingly.

Most people spend a significant portion of their lives chasing a definition of enough that belongs to someone else. The neighborhood that signals arrival. The title that confirms worth. The retirement account that reaches a number someone else named. Millard had, at some point early in his life, opted out of that particular competition. Not because he was defeated by it, but because he had looked at it honestly and decided it was not the game he wanted to play.

What he had instead was proportion. His fourteen-year-old truck was not a failure to afford a newer one. It was a choice about where his money went and what it was for. His hardware store coffee was not a consolation prize. It was a ritual he genuinely valued, with people he genuinely liked, in a community he had chosen and that had chosen him back.

The happiness researchers have a name for what Millard practiced: autonomy. The sense that your life is organized around your own values rather than borrowed ones. It turns out to be one of the strongest predictors of lasting life satisfaction, more reliable than income above a comfortable baseline, more durable than status, more sustaining than almost anything the culture markets as the path to a good life.

Millard did not know any of this. He just knew what he liked and lived accordingly.

That is, in my experience, the most practical definition of wisdom available.

The Simple Joy Story

Joy of the simple variety is not fashionable. It does not photograph well. It does not scale. It cannot be optimized, systematized, or productized into something that generates revenue. It has, as a category, almost no status in a culture that rewards complexity, intensity, and visible achievement.

It also happens to be one of the most reliable sources of genuine happiness available to human beings, accessible to almost anyone, at almost any time, at essentially no cost. The fact that it is undervalued by the culture does not make it less real. It makes it more available in the way that any undervalued thing is more available to the people who know what it is worth.

Situation

Diane did not know what it was worth. Walter the beagle was patient enough to show her.

Diane was the kind of person who kept her head down and her calendar full. She was not unhappy, exactly. She simply could not have told you, if pressed, what made her happy. That question had not come up in a while.

The change did not arrive as a crisis, a diagnosis, or a dramatic external event. It arrived, with almost comic understatement, as a dog.

Her neighbor Ruth had a beagle named Walter who required two walks a day. Ruth's hip had been troubling her, and she mentioned this one morning with the careful casualness of someone not entirely sure how to ask for help. Diane, running late with three unread messages on her phone, heard herself say she would be happy to walk Walter in the mornings. She was not sure why she said it. She said it anyway.

The first morning, she arrived with her phone, a podcast, and a route calculated for maximum efficiency. Walter had a different itinerary. He stopped at the base of the first oak tree for what Diane considered an unreasonable amount of time. He investigated a storm drain with characteristic thoroughness. He sat down briefly in the middle of the sidewalk and looked at the sky with the serene expression of a creature for whom the concept of a schedule did not exist.

Turning Point

She put the podcast away after the third morning.

By the third week, she had noticed the way the light came through the oak trees at that particular hour. She had learned the name of the man who sat on his porch every morning and lifted his coffee cup slightly as they passed. She was outside. She was moving slowly. She had nowhere to be for forty minutes. She was, without having planned it or optimized it in any way, content.

Simple joy does not announce itself or compete for attention. It waits patiently and without resentment for the moment when a person slows down enough to be present to what is actually in front of them.

The joy was never somewhere else. It was always on the same street she was already walking down. She just had to stop calculating the route long enough to look around.

Walter could not be argued with, outpaced, or scheduled around. He was the constraint that became the teacher, and the teacher had no interest in her podcast or her efficiency metrics or the four o'clock call she was perpetually rescheduling. He had interests of his own, and they were entirely concerned with the present moment: this tree, this storm drain, this patch of morning light. His curriculum was presence, taught four mornings a week at whatever pace the oak trees required.

The application for anyone reading this is not that you need a beagle, though Walter would probably argue otherwise. It is that the invitation to simple joy is being extended to you constantly, in the form of small things happening on whatever street you are already walking down. The man lifting his coffee cup. The light at a particular hour. The specific comedy of two creatures engaged in a ritual that never resolves and continues anyway. These are not small things dressed up as significant ones. They are significant things that have been moving too fast to register.

Slow down enough to receive them. That is the whole assignment.

Lesson

Diane did not discover happiness in the walks with Walter. She rediscovered it. It had been present the whole time, running alongside her ordinary days, waiting to be noticed. What the walks gave her was not joy itself but the conditions under which joy became visible: slowness, repetition, and a companion who had no agenda beyond the next interesting smell.

This is what simple joy actually requires. Not extraordinary circumstances. Not the arrival of something long awaited. Just the willingness to be present to what is already there, in the form it has actually taken rather than the form you were expecting.

The storm drain was not a beautiful thing. It was a drain. Walter found it endlessly fascinating. Diane, watching him, found herself smiling at a drain, which is not something she would have predicted about herself at this stage of her life, and which turned out to be one of the small mercies of it.

Simple joy does not ask much of us. It asks only that we slow down enough to receive it, which is harder than it sounds in a culture that mistakes busyness for meaning and acceleration for progress. The walk that takes twice as long because the dog stopped at something is not a disrupted walk. It is the walk. The interruption is the point.

Walter is gone now, as dogs eventually go, which is one of the quiet griefs of loving them. But Diane still takes the walks. A little slower now. Still paying attention.

The drain is still there.

Chapter 19

COMMUNITY AND BELONGING

Belonging is one of the least replaceable experiences in human life. People can survive for some time without it. They do not flourish there. In the later chapters of life, especially after work structures fade and children launch, the need for belonging does not diminish. It often becomes more visible.

The research on loneliness in older adults is among the most troubling findings in the science of human well-being. People over sixty report higher rates of social isolation than almost any other age group, despite having more time available for connection than they have had since childhood. The irony is exact and painful: the season of life when the calendar finally opens up is often the season when the relationships that filled it have thinned, moved away, or been lost altogether. The children are grown. The colleagues are retired. The friendships built around shared circumstance, the school, the office, the neighborhood of a particular decade, have been quietly interrupted by the accumulation of change.

What fills that space is not automatic. It requires, in many cases, the same deliberate effort that building a career once required. The people who do it, who actively construct community in the later chapters of their lives, tend to be among the happiest people of their age. The ones who wait for community to find them tend to wait a long time.

George and Lillian did not set out to build a community. They set out to find something to do on Tuesday mornings.

Situation

They had been married for forty-one years when George retired from the engineering firm where he had spent his entire career. Lillian had retired two years earlier from the school district where she had taught fourth grade for twenty-seven years. They were, by any reasonable measure, prepared for retirement. The finances were in order. The house was paid for. The grandchildren were close enough to visit regularly and far enough away that the visits remained genuinely enjoyable.

What they had not prepared for was the particular silence of a Tuesday morning with nowhere to be.

The first six months were pleasant enough. They traveled, as planned. They visited the children, as planned. They worked through the accumulated list of home projects that decades of busy schedules had deferred. George played golf. Lillian read more than she had read in years. They were, by their own description, fine.

Fine was not, they began to realize, the same as full.

What was missing was not activity. It was people. Specifically, the daily, reliable, low stakes contact with other people that the workplace and the school had provided without either of them ever having to think about it. The conversations that happened simply because you were in the same building as someone else. The colleague who stopped by your desk. The parent who caught you in the school parking lot. The accumulated texture of connection that had been, for most of their adult lives, a byproduct of the work rather than something they had deliberately constructed.

Without the work, the byproduct had disappeared. And they had not known it was load bearing until it was gone.

Turning Point

It was Lillian who found the woodworking class. She had no particular interest in woodworking and said so to George when she showed him the community center brochure. What she had interest in, she told him, was doing something on Tuesday mornings that involved other people. The subject matter was secondary.

George went because she asked, which is the reason most men of his generation try most new things, and because six months of fine had made him willing to try almost anything that might improve on it.

The class was twelve people. Most of them were in their sixties and seventies. None of them were particularly skilled at woodworking, which turned out to be the point. There is something that happens in a room full of people who are all equally bad at something: the usual social hierarchies dissolve, and what replaces them is a kind of collaborative incompetence that produces, against all expectations, genuine warmth.

By the third Tuesday, George and Lillian knew everyone's name. By the sixth, they had been invited to dinner by a couple named Frank and Louise who lived three miles away and whom they had somehow never encountered in forty years of living in the same city. By the end of the first year, the Tuesday class had generated a Saturday morning coffee group, a walking club that met three times a week, and a standing monthly dinner that rotated houses.

None of this had been the goal. The goal had been to find something to do on Tuesday mornings. What they found instead was a community, built from scratch, in the last quarter of their lives, from a subject matter neither of them particularly cared about and from the reliable magic of showing up in the same room as other people on a regular basis.

Lesson

George and Lillian will tell you, if you ask them, that the woodworking class was not really about woodworking. This is perhaps the understatement of their retirement. The woodworking class was about the discovery, made at sixty-three and sixty-five, that community does not maintain itself and does not arrive on its own, but that it is also not particularly difficult to build if you are willing to show up somewhere, repeatedly, among people who are also willing to show up.

The relationships that developed from those Tuesday mornings became, in relatively short order, among the most important in their lives. Not because they were old friendships with decades of shared history. Because they were present ones. Built from the material of the current chapter rather than borrowed from a chapter that had already closed. The conversations at Frank and Louise's dinner table were not conversations about what things used to be like. They were conversations about what things are like now, which turns out to be a different and more nourishing kind.

The lesson is not subtle: if you are in a season of life where the natural structures that once generated connection have dissolved, you will need to build new ones deliberately. The subject matter is secondary. The consistency is everything. Show up somewhere, regularly, among people who are also showing up. Let the community be a byproduct of the showing up, the way it always was, just with you doing the arranging this time, rather than the institution doing it for you.

George built a small bookshelf in that first year of the class. It is slightly uneven, and one of the shelves has a visible gap that he never quite corrected. It sits in their living room and holds, among other things, the photograph from Frank and Louise's last dinner, which eleven people attended on a rainy Saturday in October, and which lasted until nearly midnight.

He considers it one of the finest things he has ever made.

The Watch

The crew of the night shift on the USS Farragut did not choose each other.

This is worth establishing at the outset, because the story of what developed among them is sometimes mistaken for the story of compatible people who got lucky. It was not that. It was the story of seven people who were assigned to the same space at the same hours under conditions that did not accommodate the luxury of incompatibility, and who discovered, under those conditions, something that most people spend their whole lives looking for in more comfortable circumstances.

The seven of them covered the twelve-to-four watch, which sounds tolerable until you understand that the twelve-to-four watch runs from midnight to four in the morning and then you do your daily duties until around 6 PM, which means you are never sleeping at the right time and always eating at the wrong one and perpetually existing at a slight remove from the natural rhythms of the world above the waterline. The rest of the crew called it the mid-watch. The seven people who stood it called it, among themselves, simply the watch, the way people name the thing they share.

Marcus was the officer of the watch, twenty-six years old, eighteen months out of the Naval Academy, absolutely certain he was more prepared than he was and aware of this certainty in the way that twenty-six-year-olds are occasionally aware of their own overconfidence, which is to say intermittently and incompletely. Beside him at various stations: Petty Officer Chen, who had been on submarines for nine years and who possessed the particular quality of competence that makes rank irrelevant; Torres and Walsh, both second-class petty officers who had developed a wordless communication so efficient that the rest of the watch had stopped trying to follow it; a young seaman named Briggs who was technically the most junior person on the watch and who had, for reasons that took Marcus several weeks to fully appreciate, the steadiest hands and the calmest disposition of anyone in the space; the engineman they all called Soup, whose actual last name was Campell, which everyone agreed was not his fault; and a petty officer named Rios who had been passed over for promotion twice and who performed her duties with a focused excellence that Marcus eventually understood was not despite the disappointments but in some complicated way because of them.

Seven people. Twelve to four. Ninety feet underwater, in the dark, responsible for each other and for the vessel and for the mission, which Marcus was not at liberty to discuss in detail and which he carried with a weight that he had not expected and that, over time, he came to be grateful for.

The thing about the watch, Marcus would say later, was the honesty.

Not the emotional kind, not the kind that requires vulnerability and careful conversation, and the creation of the right conditions. The operational kind. The kind that is enforced by physics.

When you are responsible for a submarine at midnight, at depth, with seven people whose lives and whose mission depend on accurate information delivered in real time, there is no space for the ordinary social fictions that make above-ground life livable. You cannot tell Marcus what he wants to hear about the reactor status. You cannot soften a reading that needs to be reported sharply. You cannot manage upward, or present well, or find the diplomatic framing that makes a problem sound smaller than it is. The problem is what it is. You say what it is. He responds to what it is. Everyone moves.

This operational honesty, practiced under pressure over months, does something to the people who practice it together. It builds a particular kind of trust that Marcus had not encountered before and has not fully encountered since. Not the trust that comes from liking someone or finding them agreeable or sharing a worldview. The trust that comes from knowing, empirically and repeatedly, that when this person tells you something, it is what they actually believe and what they have actually observed. The trust that comes from having been in the difficult situation enough times to know how each person moves through it.

You learn things about people in the dark, at depth, at midnight, that you cannot learn in any other conditions. You learn what they are when they are tired, and the problem is real, and there is no audience for how they handle it. That knowledge, accumulated over the length of a deployment, is a different kind of knowing than the kind available in ordinary life.

The deployment lasted seven months. By the third month, the watch had developed its own language, its own rhythms, its own internal economy of humor that functioned as pressure relief and would have been incomprehensible to anyone outside the space.

Chen had a thing he did with his eyebrows when a reading came in that required attention but not alarm, a slight elevation on the left side only, which Marcus learned to read as noteworthy, not critical, and handle it. Walsh and Torres had refined their wordless communication to the point that they could resolve routine situations with a look, which initially unnerved Marcus, and which he eventually came to find one of the most elegant things he had ever watched two people do. Briggs, the most junior, had an instinct for the moment when tension was building and needed to be punctured, and could do it with a single dry observation that landed without making anyone feel managed.

Rios brought coffee at 0200 every night without being asked. Not only to Marcus. To whoever was at whatever station, without ceremony or commentary, in the particular way of someone who has decided that this is a thing they do and requires no further discussion. Marcus never thanked her for this in words. He thanked her by noticing it, which was, he suspected, what she wanted.

Soup told the same three stories on rotation, always with slight variations, and everyone pretended each iteration was the first time they had heard it. This was a gift they gave him. He gave them other things in return.

The watch ended, not the individual watches but the deployment, the seven months, and the crew returned to port, and the seven people went in seven directions, as naval personnel do, and the watch was over in the way that watches end.

Marcus has stayed in contact with Chen, who left the Navy two years later and now runs a maintenance operation in Baton Rouge and, whom Marcus calls three or four times a year with no particular agenda. He exchanged messages with Rios at holidays for several years and then lost the thread in the way that threads are lost, without either of them deciding to lose it. He has no contact information for Soup, or Briggs, or Walsh.

Torres, he ran into once, entirely by accident, in an airport in Houston, fifteen years after the deployment. They recognized each other across a crowded gate area in the specific way that people recognize each other when the shared experience was unusual enough to make the other person's face permanently available. They had coffee for forty minutes. They talked about the watch. They talked about almost nothing else, which is to say they talked about the only thing that mattered, and when they boarded their separate flights, Marcus felt something he had not fully resolved into a sentence.

Something like: that was real. Whatever else has been real, that was real.

What the watch gave seven people who did not choose each other was a form of belonging that Marcus has spent the subsequent decades trying to accurately describe and has not quite managed.

It was not friendship exactly, though it was that too. It was not camaraderie exactly, though it was that too. It was something more specific: the experience of being fully known in a context that mattered, by people who had no reason to perform for you and no incentive to soften what they saw, and who showed up anyway, every night, twelve to four, and brought the coffee and read the eyebrows and told the same three stories and kept the submarine and each other in the dark and the cold and the particular silence of the deep water, and did all of this without ever making a speech about it.

Marcus has been in many rooms since the watch. Boardrooms and classrooms and conference rooms and the ordinary rooms of a life that has been, by most measures, a good one.

He has never been in a room where the trust came pre-installed.

In every other room, it had to be built. It could be built. He knew how, because of the watch. But it always had to be built, which meant it was always, in some way, chosen, by people who had the option of choosing otherwise, in conditions that permitted a certain amount of comfortable distance.

The watch had not permitted comfortable distance. Seven people, twelve to four, ninety feet down. Distance is a luxury the dark water does not offer.

He has come to believe that this is the condition under which the deepest belonging is formed: not when people choose each other under favorable conditions, but when circumstances remove the option of not choosing, and the people turn toward each other anyway, and discover in that turning something they did not know they were looking for.

He is grateful for the watch. He is grateful for Chen and Torres and Rios and Walsh and Briggs and Soup, in whatever order they now occupy in a life that has moved well past the deployment.

He is grateful, most of all, for what seven people who did not choose each other discovered together, at midnight, at depth, in the dark.

That some of the most important rooms you ever inhabit are the ones you did not pick, with the people who were simply there, doing what needed to be done, beside you.

Chapter 20

LOSS, GRIEF, AND JOY TOGETHER

The Anniversary

My parents were supposed to go in a certain order.

This is not a morbid observation. It is the kind of practical arithmetic that adult children do when their parents are aging, the quiet accounting of health and age and circumstance that produces a working theory about how things will unfold. My father developed dementia in his late seventies, the particular variety known as Sundowner's syndrome, which caused him to become active and disoriented in the evening hours, rising to go about the routines of his day at the times when the day was supposed to be over. He would dress for work in the middle of the night. He would try to leave for appointments that had happened decades ago. The evening became dangerous in ways that the family could no longer manage at home, and he was admitted to a managed care facility where he would be safe and where the staff understood the particular geography of a mind that had lost its sense of time.

My mother remained at home. She had some minor COPD, the kind that requires management rather than alarm, and she was otherwise, at eighty-five, in reasonable health. She was sharp. She was herself. She was, by any honest assessment, the one we expected to be with us longer.

The arithmetic, as it turned out, was wrong.

My mother was of Irish descent, which in our family was not simply an ethnic fact but a living tradition carried forward with genuine conviction. She celebrated being Irish the way some people celebrate religion, which is to say consistently, joyfully, and with particular intensity on the designated holy days.

The holiest of those days, for her, was St. Patrick's Day.

For years, her celebration centered on her best friend, a woman who played the piano beautifully and who hosted a St. Patrick's Day party at her home that my mother looked forward to the way a child looks forward to Christmas. The music, the company, the particular warmth of a room full of people who are glad to be exactly where they are, my mother lived for that day and for what it represented.

Her friend died about three years before my mother did.

I have thought about that loss and what it meant to my mother. The party stopped. The piano was silent on St. Patrick's Day. Something that had been a pillar of her year was simply gone, and she was eighty-two years old, and her husband was in a memory care facility, and the world she had built over the course of a long life was becoming smaller in the way that the worlds of the very old become smaller, one beloved person at a time.

Her health deteriorated rapidly in the early spring of her eighty-fifth year. She passed away in early March.

We were sad. Of course, we were sad. She was our mother and she was gone, and the sadness was real and appropriate, and we did not try to manage it into something more comfortable than it was.

And then one of my siblings said the thing that changed how we held it. She wanted to get to heaven for St. Patrick's Day.

Her friend was there. The piano was there. The party had moved, that was all, moved to a place my mother was now headed, at the time of year she would have chosen if choosing had been available to her, just in time for the celebration she had been missing for three years.

I cannot tell you with certainty that this is what happened, because certainty about such things is not available to the living. What I can tell you is that it is true in the way that the best explanations are true: it fits. It fits everything we knew about her, everything she loved, the timing that could not have been more precisely her if she had arranged it herself.

We held onto that.

My father outlasted our revised arithmetic as well.

He held on through the spring and into the summer, past the point where the doctors had gently suggested we prepare ourselves, past the point where the preparation had been made and remade. He was not well. But he was still there, in whatever diminished and altered way a person with advanced dementia is still there, and he stayed through June and into July.

He passed away in July. One of my siblings, doing the arithmetic again, noticed the date.

His wedding anniversary was the following day.

He had been trying to get there, too. Not away from us, or not only away from us, but toward her. Toward the anniversary they had shared for decades. Toward the woman who had gone ahead of him in March and who was, if you believe what we believe, waiting for him somewhere with a party already in progress and a piano being played by someone with very talented hands.

Both of our parents were gone. It was a sad time. I will not dress it as anything other than what it was. But it was also held in the light of what my siblings had noticed, something else alongside the sadness. Something that did not cancel the grief but sat with it, the way joy and sorrow can sit together in the same room when you let them. The idea that the two people who had given us our beginning were now together for their anniversary, that they had each found their way to the other in their own time and in their own way, with a precision that felt less like coincidence and more like intention.

My mother made it for St. Patrick's Day. My father made it for the anniversary. They were always, in every way that mattered, going to the same place.

The Lesson

Loss is not a problem to be solved. It is an experience to be moved through, and the moving through it is one of the most universal and least discussed of human experiences. We are, as a culture, better at avoiding the subject than at sitting with it honestly.

What my family discovered in those two losses, offered close together in the same year, is something I want to name carefully because it is easily misunderstood: grief and joy are not opposites. They are not a toggle switch where the presence of one requires the absence of the other. They can, and in the richest human experiences often do, occupy the same space at the same time.

The grief was real. My parents were gone, and we missed them, and the missing did not resolve quickly and does not resolve completely even now. That is the nature of loving people across a long-shared life and then losing them.

The joy was also real. The image of my mother arriving in time for a party she had been missing for three years. The image of my father, holding on with the particular stubbornness of a man who had things to do, making it to his anniversary. The understanding that what looked like leaving was also, from another angle, arriving, that the two people who had loved each other long enough to share sixty-plus years and an anniversary were together again.

Neither the grief nor the joy is more true than the other. Both are true completely and simultaneously, which is the way human experience actually works when we allow it to, rather than insisting that we feel only one thing at a time.

The sun came up the morning after my father passed. It came up the morning after my mother passed. On one of those mornings, somewhere we cannot see, a party was just getting started. On another, an anniversary was being celebrated.

I believe that. It fits everything I knew about them.

And in the believing, the grief that was real and the joy that was also real found a way to sit together, and the sitting together made both more bearable and both more true.

Chapter 21

THE HAPPINESS WE DIDN'T EXPECT

There is a happiness available in the later chapters of a life that the earlier ones simply cannot produce, not because anything was wrong with the earlier ones, but because this particular happiness requires what only time can provide: the accumulated experience of having wanted many things, received some of them, lost some of them, and arrived, finally, at a reasonably accurate understanding of which ones actually mattered.

The stories in the previous chapters were not about grand reinventions. They were about recognition. A couple recognizing that the person they chose was still there beneath the logistics of family life. A woman recognizing that joy had been waiting on the same sidewalks she had walked for years. A retired couple recognizing that community would not appear automatically and deciding, without making a speech about it, to build one. A man recognizing that a small, specific life can be richer than an impressive, restless one.

The common thread is not age by itself. Plenty of people grow older without growing clearer. The common thread is a willingness to be corrected by life. To let experience refine desire. To stop assuming that the loudest forms of happiness are the deepest ones.

What younger people often misunderstand about later-life happiness is that it is not merely quieter. It is more accurate. It has been tested by disappointment, recalibrated by loss, softened by love, and stripped of some illusions that make earlier seasons more frantic than they need to be. It is less interested in performance and more interested in presence. Less fascinated by accumulation and more attentive to what remains. Less concerned with being impressive and more concerned with being available.

This is one reason grandparents can be such a gift when they are at their best. They are not usually trying to win anymore. They are free to notice. They can sit on the floor longer. Listen more patiently. Tell the story without editing out the parts that matter most. The late-life gift is not only wisdom. It is spaciousness.

There is also a warning embedded here. None of this arrives automatically. People do not drift into contentment any more than they drift into physical fitness. Some become narrower with age, more anxious, more isolated, more convinced that the best parts are behind them. The later chapters amplify what has been practiced earlier. If gratitude has been practiced, later life grows sweeter. If comparison has been practiced, later life can grow bitter. If service has been practiced, later life remains full of purpose. If people have been neglected, the absence becomes louder.

That is why these chapters matter before we get there. The life we are building now is the life we will inhabit then.

I have come to believe that one of the greatest mercies in life is that happiness keeps changing form. It meets us differently at twenty-five than it does at forty-five. It meets us differently at sixty-five than it did at thirty. This is not inconsistency. It is grace. The forms of joy appropriate to one chapter are not always sufficient for the next, and life, if we are paying attention, keeps offering revised invitations.

The invitation in the later chapters is simple. Slow down enough to recognize what remains. Protect the relationships that have earned your trust. Build new forms of belonging where the old ones have dissolved. Be useful to someone. Let ordinary joy count. Refuse the lie that because some doors have closed, the house itself is empty.

Some of the best things in a life are the ones we did not plan. Not because planning is foolish, but because planning is limited. It can only work with what we currently know how to desire. Happiness often arrives from beyond that range. It enters through a neighbor, a dog, a Tuesday night reservation, a woodworking class, a grandchild, a long-delayed quiet, a second career, a slower morning, a different definition of enough.

That is the happiness we did not expect. It is not lesser because it was unplanned. It is often deeper because it was received.

Final Chapter

TOMORROW ALWAYS COMES

Every book about happiness eventually has to answer a question it has been circling for the whole length of itself: So, what do I actually do?

Not the abstract version of the question. The practical one. The version asked by someone who has read to the end and found themselves genuinely moved by some of it, mildly challenged by some of it, and now sitting with the particular restlessness of a person who has been shown something true and is trying to figure out what to do with it before the feeling fades and Tuesday arrives with its usual insistence.

I want to try to answer that question directly, before I close.

What the Journey Covered

We began with a woman who worried about everything. She was not unusual. She was, in many ways, representative of the way most of us move through the world when we have not yet found the phrase, or the practice, or the morning, or the person, that helps us set the worry down long enough to see what is actually there.

Her phrase was seven words. The sun will come up tomorrow. It did not solve her problems. It did not prevent the marriages that failed or spare her the difficulties her children had to navigate. What it did, slowly and over time, was shift the relationship between the worry and the life. The worry was still there. But it stopped being the whole story. The life, with all its unexpected outcomes and unplanned detours, turned out to be bigger than the worry. Her children became people she was proud of. She found peace near her grandchildren. The life she ended up with was not the one she had spent years anxiously constructing in her imagination. It was better.

That is the whole argument of this book, stated plainly: the life actually available to us is almost always larger than the one our worry has been rehearsing. The stops we didn't plan are often the ones that matter most. The happiness we find is rarely the happiness we were specifically looking for.

Seven Threads Worth Carrying

Part III of this book explored seven qualities that drive happiness: perspective, relationships, purpose, gratitude, resilience, humor, and service. I want to revisit each of them briefly, not to summarize what the chapters said, but to distill what I have come to believe, after a long career of working with people and a longer life of living alongside them, is the single most useful thing to know about each one.

On perspective: You cannot always change what is happening. You can almost always change the lens through which you view it. The pilots on that flight back to Charlotte were not in a better situation than the passengers. They were in a better relationship with the situation. That relationship is available to you in almost any circumstance you will face. The question is whether you will choose it.

On relationships: The people who show up are the people who matter. Not the ones who mean to, not the ones who send thoughtful messages from a comfortable distance, not the ones who care in theory. The ones who get in the car. If you want to know what your relationships are actually made of, ask yourself how often you get in the car. And ask yourself who you know right now that you should be getting in the car for.

On purpose: It does not retire on schedule, and it does not require dramatic reinvention. It requires the honest answer to a simple question: what have I kept coming back to, even when I was doing something else? That answer is usually short. It is usually already true. It is usually pointing somewhere worth going.

On gratitude: Take the inventory. Not the inventory of what is gone, which takes care of itself. The inventory of what remains. Most people, when they do this honestly, are surprised by how much is on the list. The list does not erase the losses. But it refuses to let the losses be the only accounting.

On resilience: You have survived everything that has come for you so far. That is a one hundred percent success rate, measured correctly. The next difficult thing will require the same thing the previous ones required: the decision, made in the absence of certainty, to keep going. That decision is available to you. It has always been available to you. It will be available tomorrow.

On humor: Laughter is not the opposite of seriousness. It is the maintenance that makes sustained seriousness possible. The people around you are carrying more than they show. A room that has room for laughter is a room where people can keep going. Be the person who refuses to let fear have the whole room to itself.

On service: A life organized entirely around personal comfort becomes, over time, strangely small. When it includes contribution, it expands. The question is not whether you have time to be useful to someone else. The question is what you are waiting for before you begin. The answer to that question is almost always: nothing.

The Stops I Would Revisit

If I could go back to any stop along the way and sit with it a little longer, I would go back to the submarine. Not because it was the most comfortable stop, it was not. Because the crew I served with there demonstrated something I have spent the rest of my career trying to articulate and have never quite matched: a collective commitment to competence and to each other that made both the work and the people better than either would have been apart. I have worked in a great many organizations since those years. I have never stopped using what I learned on that boat as the standard against which I measure what a real team looks like.

I would go back to the morning of the blizzard, driving toward a hospital through roads that had no business being driven on, because that was the morning I learned what motivation actually feels like when it is connected to something larger than yourself. We were going to make it because there was no acceptable alternative. Most of the best things I have ever done in my professional life were done in some version of that spirit.

I would go back to the kitchen table where my father sat with grandchildren who adored him, not for the version of him that I had grieved, but for the one sitting there. I would sit across from that man and pay attention to what he had figured out that I was still working on. I would not try to get the old version back. I would learn from the new one while the learning was still available.

I would go back to the parking lot in August where we dropped our daughter off for college, not to change anything about the day, but to tell myself that the napkins in the glove compartment are enough. That the long silences and the quiet Saturday dinners that follow are not the end of something. They are the beginning of a different something, and the different something has its own rewards, its own discoveries, its own Tuesday nights that become the best part of the week.

What the Sun Actually Means

I have been saying this phrase for most of my adult life. It started as a piece of comfort offered to someone who needed it. It became, over time, something I have come to believe in a way that goes well beyond comfort.

The sun will come up tomorrow is not optimism. Optimism is the belief that things will probably work out well. This is something more specific than that. It is the belief that tomorrow will arrive regardless of how tonight feels, that the day that follows any night is a new point of departure, that the circumstances of the present moment are never the final word on what is possible.

I have lived through nights that made tomorrow feel doubtful. I imagine you have too. The career that collapsed. The relationship that ended. The diagnosis that changed the terms of everything. The loss that arrived without warning and stayed beyond what felt survivable. These things are real, and this phrase does not diminish them. What it does is refuse to let them be the last word.

The sun came up after every one of those nights. And in the day that followed, something was possible that had not been possible the night before, even if that something was only the decision to take the next step. That decision, taken in the morning, is everything. It is where every recovery begins. It is where every new chapter starts. It is where the story continues, which is the only thing required of it.

One Last Thing

I wrote this book because a colleague told me I was one of the happiest people they knew and suggested I write about it. I thought it was an interesting idea and set it aside. Then I woke up in the middle of the night with the book in my head and could not get it back out until I had put it on the page.

What I hope you take from it is not a system or a method or a set of principles to be implemented. Those things have their place. This is not that book. What I hope you take is something quieter and more durable: the recognition that the happiness available to you is larger than the version you have been settling for, that the stops you did not plan are worth your full attention, and that the phrase is true in ways that take a lifetime to fully appreciate.

The woman from the introduction found her peace. The children she worried about became people worth being proud of. The grandchildren she wondered if she would ever get to know are growing up now in a home where she is present, and glad to be there, and no longer spending the morning in a hospital she constructed overnight in her imagination.

That is what the sun coming up looks like, in practice. Not dramatic. Not the ending of a movie. Just a person, standing in an ordinary morning, present enough to appreciate it.

I hope that is where this book leaves you.

The sun will come up tomorrow. It always has.

Be there for it.

THE SUNRISE MANIFESTO

These are not rules. They are not a program. They are simply truths that a long life, a great deal of listening, and considerable reflection have made it difficult to argue with.

1. Life rarely follows the plan we imagine. This is not a problem to be solved. It is the nature of a life fully lived.
2. Most of the things we worry about never happen. The rest we are more capable of handling than we feared.
3. How we start the day shapes how we experience the day. Choose carefully what you let in before 8 a.m.
4. Perspective changes everything. Two people in identical circumstances will experience them entirely differently depending on where they choose to direct their attention.
5. Relationships are the foundation of happiness. The people who show up matter more than the people who mean to.
6. Purpose gives direction to our days. It does not retire on schedule. It is available at every age to anyone willing to keep asking for it.
7. Gratitude reveals what is already good. It is not a feeling we wait for. It is a decision about where to direct attention.
8. Resilience is stronger than circumstance. It is not the absence of struggle. It is the decision to keep skating through it.

9. Happiness often appears in unexpected places. Pay attention at the stops. That is where it lives.
10. Tomorrow always arrives. What we choose to do with the day it brings is entirely ours.

THE HAPPINESS PROFILE

A Personal Survey

This survey is designed to help you understand your current relationship with five of the seven qualities explored in Part III of this book: Perspective, Relationships, Purpose, Gratitude, and Resilience. Humor and Service, while essential drivers of happiness, are best experienced and practiced rather than scored.

There are no right or wrong answers. Answer honestly based on how you actually live, not how you aspire to live. The value of this survey is not in the score itself but in what it reveals about where you are thriving and where you have the most room to grow.

Complete the survey before reading the book to establish a baseline. Complete it again afterward to see what has shifted. Some people find it useful to revisit it annually.

Rating Scale

1 = Rarely or never 2 = Occasionally 3 = Sometimes 4 = Often 5 = Almost always

Section 1: Perspective

When something goes wrong, I am able to find a constructive way to look at it.
Rating: ____

I recognize when my interpretation of a situation may be making it worse than it actually is.
Rating: ____

I can hold disappointment without letting it define how I experience the rest of my day.
Rating: ____

I am able to see setbacks as potential redirections rather than final verdicts.
Rating: ____

Section 1 Total: ____ (out of 20)

Section 2: Relationships
I have people in my life I can call on when things are genuinely difficult.
Rating: ____

I make time for the relationships that matter most to me, even when life is busy.
Rating: ____

I show up for others in the ways I hope they would show up for me.
Rating: ____

My closest relationships feel genuinely reciprocal, built on presence rather than convenience.
Rating: ____

Section 2 Total: ____ (out of 20)

Section 3: Purpose
I have a clear sense of why the work I do matters beyond a paycheck.
Rating: ____

I regularly engage in activities that make me lose track of time because I am so absorbed in them.
Rating: ____

I feel that my daily life is connected to something larger than my own immediate needs.
Rating: ____

I can answer the question 'What have I kept coming back to, even when I was doing something else?' with a clear and honest answer.
Rating: ____

Section 3 Total: ____ (out of 20)

Section 4: Gratitude

I regularly notice and appreciate things in my daily life that are going well.
Rating: ____

When I face a loss or disappointment, I am still able to identify what remains and what I am grateful for.
Rating: ____

I express appreciation to the people in my life rather than assuming they know how I feel.
Rating: ____

I spend more mental energy on what I have than on what I lack.
Rating: ____

Section 4 Total: ____ (out of 20)

Section 5: Resilience

When something goes wrong, I am able to recover and move forward without dwelling on it excessively.
Rating: ____

I have navigated significant setbacks in my life and emerged from them without lasting bitterness.
Rating: ____

When I face a difficult situation, I make the decision to keep going even when the outcome is uncertain.
Rating: ____

I believe that most difficult chapters in my life have eventually led somewhere meaningful.
Rating: ____

Section 5 Total: ____ (out of 20)

Your Happiness Profile Score
Add your five section totals together for your overall score.
Perspective: ____ Relationships: ____ Purpose: ____ Gratitude: ____ Resilience: ____
Overall Score: ____ (out of 100)

Interpreting Your Score

80 to 100: You are actively cultivating happiness across most dimensions of your life. The chapters in this book will reinforce what you are already doing well and may illuminate a dimension or two worth strengthening further.

60 to 79: You have a solid foundation. Most of the drivers of happiness are present in your life in meaningful ways. Look at which section scored lowest. That chapter holds the most opportunity for you right now.

40 to 59: Some areas of your life are working well and others need deliberate attention. The good news is that the drivers of happiness are learnable and practicable. Start with the section that scored lowest and read that chapter first.

Below 40: This book arrived at the right time. Be honest with yourself about which dimensions are most depleted and approach each chapter as a genuine invitation rather than a review of things you already know. Happiness is not a fixed trait. It is a practice, and practices can be developed at any stage of life.

Note your five section scores here so you can compare them after finishing the book. The overall number matters less than the pattern. Where are you strongest? Where is the most room to grow? Those answers point you toward the chapters that will serve you most.

A READER'S GUIDE

Discussion Questions

These questions are designed for book clubs, leadership groups, corporate wellness programs, or personal reflection. They are organized by part and updated to match this revised manuscript structure.

Introduction and Opening Reflections

1. The author describes a phrase he has been saying for most of his adult life: 'The sun will come up tomorrow.' Is there a phrase or belief that has played a similar role in your life?
2. The woman in the Introduction worried about almost everything, yet her children grew up to build remarkable lives. Has worry ever served as a substitute for trust or perspective in your own life?
3. The author asks whether he became successful and then happy, or happy first. How would you answer that question about your own life?
4. He describes happiness as something we choose rather than something that happens to us. Do you agree? Where does choice end and circumstance begin?

Part I: The Foundation of Happiness

5. Marcus in Chapter 1 keeps moving the goalpost for his own happiness. What is your current 'I'll be happy when ...'?

What would it mean to stop and test whether that assumption is even true?

6. Chapter 2 argues that comparison gives us truth without context. Where in your life are you most tempted to compare your reality to someone else's excerpt?
7. Karen's eleven-minute worry spiral in Chapter 3 is played partly for comedy, but the insight is serious: the catastrophe was cancelled and the suffering was not. What forms of pre-suffering are most common in your own mind?
8. Chapter 4 describes the effect of starting the day with the local news. What is the first thing you let into your mind most mornings, and what effect does it have on the rest of the day?
9. If you were to redesign your morning routine around the idea that the morning is where the day is won or lost, what would you change?
10. Chapter 5 asks what money is for. In your own life, where has money created fear, and where has it created freedom, dignity, or peace?
11. Chapter 6 argues that faith is often discovered at the edge of what control can do. What outcome in your life are you still trying to carry that may need to be put down?

Part II: Stops Along the Way

12. The first job story is about a father who taught the value of education without ever mentioning it directly. Who in your early life taught you something foundational by example rather than lecture?
13. The Naval Academy career detour in Chapter 9 describes a failure that became a redirection. Can you

identify a closed door in your own life that later looked like mercy?

14. The Rickover story suggests that the people who hold us to the highest standards are often the ones who believe most in our potential. Has that been true in your life?
15. Chapter 8 captures the moment of holding a child for the first time, a reorganization of everything. What experience in your life changed the order of your priorities almost overnight?
16. The lost job story in Chapter 9 argues that how we handle the retraction of an opportunity often matters more than how we pursued it. How do you typically respond when something you expected does not materialize?
17. The traffic jam story in Chapter 9 is really about the things we cannot change and what we do with our response to them. What is your current I-4, the regular frustration that keeps asking who you are becoming?

Part III: The Drivers of Happiness

18. Chapter 10 on Perspective includes stories in real time and in hindsight. Which kind of perspective shift is harder for you: calming yourself in the moment or reinterpreting something later?
19. The airline story shows pilots remaining calm while holding information that would have alarmed the passengers. In your own leadership, what does it look like to project calm without becoming evasive?
20. The friend who showed up in Chapter 11 got in the car on a Saturday when he could have sent a text. Who in your life right now might need you to get in the car?

21. The question in Chapter 12, 'What have I kept coming back to, even when I was doing something else?', is one of the most useful purpose questions in the book. How would you answer it?
22. Chapter 13 on Gratitude includes the practice of taking inventory of what remains. What is currently on your list that you have been overlooking?
23. Chapter 14 on Resilience argues that surviving difficulty is not the whole story; interpreting it well matters too. Which hardship in your life now looks different in retrospect than it did while you were inside it?
24. Chapter 15 on Humor and Lightheartedness suggests that laughter does not deny difficulty; it keeps fear from having the whole room to itself. Where in your life do you most need that kind of interruption right now?

Part IV: Happiness Later in Life

25. Chapter 16 suggests that service is not self-erasure but healthy usefulness. Where in your life are you most needed in a way that gives energy rather than drains it?
26. The opening reflection of Part IV describes the happiness of releasing the blueprint you held for your children. Has life asked you to let go of a blueprint and trust the person in front of you instead?
27. Chapter 17 shows Carol and Michael rediscovering each other at a restaurant they had been meaning to try for two years. What relationship in your life would benefit from that kind of deliberate attention?
28. Chapter 18 presents both Millard's contentment and Diane's slow walks with Walter the beagle. Which simple

joys in your life have become nearly invisible through familiarity?

29. Chapter 19 argues that community rarely maintains itself automatically in later life. What structures currently generate belonging for you, and which ones may need to be built rather than inherited?
30. Chapter 20 suggests that grief and joy are not opposites but companions. Have you ever experienced a season where sorrow and gratitude, or loss and joy, occupied the same room in your life at the same time?
31. Chapter 21 suggests that later-life happiness is more accurate because it has been corrected by experience. What in your definition of a good life has become more accurate with age?

Synthesis Questions

32. Looking at your Happiness Profile scores, which of the five drivers, Perspective, Relationships, Purpose, Gratitude, or Resilience, seems strongest right now? Which seems most in need of attention?
33. The author says that the happiness available to us is almost always larger than the version our worry has been rehearsing. Do you believe that for your own life right now?
34. The book ends with a simple invitation: be there for it. What is one specific, concrete change you could make this week that would make you more available to your own life?
35. If you were to write the title of the next chapter of your own life, the one that begins the morning after finishing this book, what would it be?

APPENDIX: THE PETERSEN PHILOSOPHY

For readers who want to understand how this book fits into a larger body of work, this appendix provides the framework that connects all four books in the Petersen Philosophy.

The four dimensions of the Petersen Philosophy are Character, Style, Judgment, and Happiness. Each book explores one dimension. *The Spirit to Soar* examines Character: why we lead and who we are at our core. *Who Let the Dogs Lead?* explores Style: how we lead people and what our leadership looks like in practice. *The Facts Don't Matter* addresses Judgment: how we think and decide under pressure and uncertainty. *The Sun Will Come Up Tomorrow* completes the picture with the Happiness dimension: how we live well.

At the center of the framework are Life's Stops Along the Way, and the seven qualities that drive happiness: Perspective, Relationships, Purpose, Gratitude, Resilience, Humor, and Service. These are not abstract ideals. They are the practical, daily disciplines that separate people who endure their lives from people who genuinely enjoy them.

The diagram below shows how the four dimensions connect. None of them exists in isolation. How you live shapes how you lead. How you lead shapes how you live. The road on the cover of this book leads somewhere. So does this one.

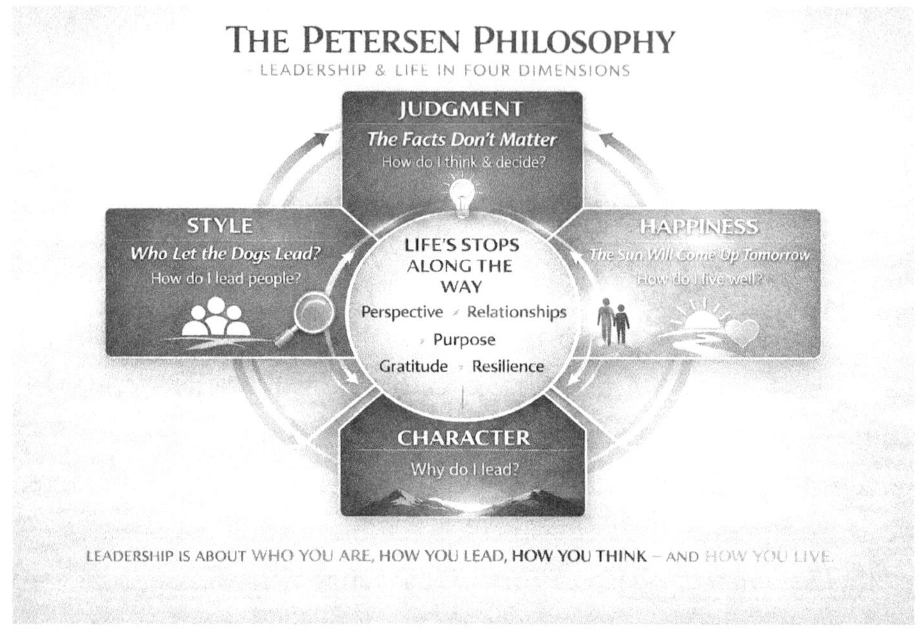
THE PETERSEN PHILOSOPHY
– LEADERSHIP & LIFE IN FOUR DIMENSIONS
JUDGMENT
The Facts Don't Matter
How do I think & decide?
STYLE
Who Let the Dogs Lead?
How do I lead people?
LIFE'S STOPS ALONG THE WAY
Perspective · Relationships · Purpose
Gratitude · Resilience
HAPPINESS
The Sun Will Come Up Tomorrow
How do I live well?
CHARACTER
Why do I lead?
LEADERSHIP IS ABOUT WHO YOU ARE, HOW YOU LEAD, HOW YOU THINK – AND HOW YOU LIVE.

ACKNOWLEDGMENTS

A book about happiness is, by its nature, a book about people. Every person whose story appears in these pages, whether by name or by the privacy of a character, contributed something that no amount of research or reflection could have provided on its own. I am grateful to all of them.

I am grateful to my wife and to our children and grandchildren, who are the living proof of everything this book tries to say. I am grateful to the colleagues, coaching clients, students, and classmates who have shared their stories and their questions with me across a career I could not have designed and would not trade.

I am grateful, in a specific way, to the woman from the Introduction, who took a throwaway phrase from a young man in her life and made it into something she could actually use. She taught me more than she knows about what it means to choose a different perspective when a different perspective is hard to find.

The sun came up again this morning. It always does.

ABOUT THE AUTHOR

Jim Petersen, PhD, is a leadership educator, executive coach, author, and retired United States Navy Captain. His career spans more than four decades and crosses an unusual range of disciplines, naval service, financial planning, sales leadership, executive recruiting, C-suite management, university teaching, and professional coaching, each one building on the last in ways he could not have planned from the starting line.

Jim graduated from the United States Naval Academy in 1976 and served as a nuclear submarine officer, qualifying submarines and completing his Engineer's Exam while serving aboard USS Indianapolis (SSN 697). During his naval career, he was ranked number one of all officer instructors at the Navy's Nuclear Power School and was later promoted to Assistant Director of that program. He received the Navy Achievement Medal at the personal direction of Admiral Hyman G. Rickover after identifying a design flaw affecting all 688 class submarines during routine maintenance, a distinction that remains one of the more improbable stories in a career full of them. He retired from the Navy and Naval Reserve as a Captain (O-6) after twenty-two years of service, having held progressive leadership positions across submarine operations, military intelligence, and the staff of Commander Atlantic Fleet.

After his military career, Jim built a thirty-five-year career in financial services with First Command Financial Services, serving military families across the country in a succession of executive and leadership roles. He holds three graduate degrees from The American College of Financial Services, including a Doctor of Philosophy in Financial and Retirement Planning, and carries more than a dozen professional designations across financial planning, estate planning, leadership, and coaching. He was inducted into The American College of Financial Services Alumni Hall of Fame in 2024 and received the FINSECA/GAMA International Cy Pick Award for Lifetime Service in 2019.

Jim currently serves as President and Owner of the Professional Business Coaches Alliance (PBCA), a global network of professional business coaches, and as CEO of Diversified Professional Coaching, LLC. He holds the Roger Hull/James S. Bingay Chair of Leadership at The American College of Financial Services and serves as an adjunct professor at the graduate level. He is a Trustee of the United States Naval Academy's Athletic and Scholarship Programs and a past Chairman of The American College Military and Veterans Advisory Council.

He is the author of six books. *From Combat to Client Service: A Guide to Hiring Military Veterans in the Financial Services Industry* and *From Combat to Corporate Life: A Guide to Hiring Military Veterans in Business* (both 2019) drew on his experience bridging military and civilian professional cultures. *The Spirit to Soar: Inspiring Life Lessons and Values for a Victorious Life* (2022) explored the foundations of character and personal leadership. *Who Let the Dogs Lead? Leadership Lessons from the Pack* and *The Facts Don't Matter: How to Stay Sane When the Truth is Optional* (both 2025) advanced the Petersen Philosophy Framework, a four-dimensional model connecting Character, Style, Judgment, and Happiness.

The Sun Will Come Up Tomorrow is his sixth book and the one he was most surprised to find himself writing.

Jim lives in Fort Worth, Texas. More information about his books, coaching work, and speaking engagements can be found at jlpeterseninc.com.

www.ingramcontent.com/pod-product-compliance
Lightning Source LLC
LaVergne TN
LVHW020709110826
845149LV00012B/2171

9781961202801